Walk by
table of thomas

EXPERIENCING
the Power of
THE CROSS

Books by
Gary Kinnaman

And Signs Shall Follow

Angels: Dark and Light

Beginner's Guide to Praise and Worship

Dumb Things Smart Christians Believe

Experiencing the Power of the Cross

Leaders That Last (with Alfred Ells)

Learning to Love the One You Marry

My Companion Through Grief

The Spirit-Filled Life Study Bible: Acts

Winning Your Spiritual Battles

EXPERIENCING
the Power of
THE CROSS

Gary Kinnaman

BETHANYHOUSE
MINNEAPOLIS, MINNESOTA

Published by Bethany House Publishers
11400 Hampshire Avenue South
Bloomington, Minnesota 55438

Bethany House Publishers is a division of
Baker Publishing Group, Grand Rapids, Michigan.

Printed in the United States of America

Library of Congress Cataloging-in-Publication Data

Kinnaman, Gary.
    Experiencing the power of the Cross : how it changes everything / by Gary Kinnaman.
        p. cm.
    Summary: "Reconnect with the reality and power of the cross to overcome life's common
struggles and gain an eternal perspective: the cross's power does not stop with reconciling
people to God, but reaches out to transform our earthly relationships as well"—Provided by
publisher.
    ISBN 0-7642-2994-X (pbk.)
    1. Christian life. 2. Jesus Christ—Crucifixion. I. Title.
    BV4509.5.K484   2005
    232.96'3—dc22   2004024193

Acknowledgments

Many thanks to many people:

To Kyle Duncan for inviting me to write for Bethany House, a most excellent Christian publisher.

To my conscientious editor, Christopher Soderstrom, who challenged and affirmed me . . . and who had to work with my unconventional style.

To my former personal assistant, Penny Jo Budd, who assisted me by word-processing most of the revisions of the first-generation manuscript.

To the Board, staff, and people of my congregation, Word of Grace Church, in Mesa, Arizona, who give me the freedom to spread the Word to the larger faith community.

To my personal assistant, Sherry Helzer, whose devotion to God and her work take a lot of pressure off my life.

And to Marilyn, my dear wife of thirty-three years and mother of our three great kids, for everything she has to put up with in my life. I'm a pastor. She's a saint. She loves the Cross of Christ and lives it.

GARY KINNAMAN is the senior pastor of Word of Grace Church (*www.wordofgrace.org*) near Phoenix. He has been instrumental in planting several other churches in Arizona, is a popular conference speaker, and has written several books, including the bestseller *Angels: Dark and Light.* Gary and his wife have three adult children and make their home in Arizona.

Contents

PART ONE

Crossing Gate

CHAPTER ONE

Love Like You Can't Imagine

"It was the worst day of my life," he told me.

Knowing my brother David, I'd have to agree.

The story actually began several years earlier, when he and his wife, Tonya, adopted two children from a Russian orphanage. They have two almost-grown kids of their own, but they'd always wanted a larger family. Through a series of extraordinary circumstances, Nicholas (age 11, they think) and Natasha (6), half-siblings, became available through an agency bringing homeless children from Russia to stable families in the States.

A year before the official adoption, the children came for an extended visit, a test run, so my brother and his wife (as well as other prospective families) could get a feel for kids who needed homes. Neither Nick nor Natasha spoke a word of English, nor had they ever experienced anything like those first weeks in America.

David and Tonya took them everywhere, including Disneyland, but the grocery store was a magic kingdom. On their first visit to

Albertsons, as my brother pulled gallons of 2% from the milk case, Natasha screamed wildly as she threw her little arms around those white frosty jugs. And you should have seen them eat fruit. Forget about ice cream, candy, and other junk food—they gorged themselves on bananas. One night the two of them devoured an entire average-sized watermelon!

Feeling a deep sense of God's leading—and after lengthy conversations with friends and family—David and Tonya decided to make Nicholas and Natasha their own. Even so, everyone cried their good-byes at the airport, because my brother and sister-in-law didn't tell the kids about their plans. Too many things could still go wrong. A year and $25,000 in fees later,[1] after two weeks and several court appearances in Russia, David and Tonya returned home with their new children. They arrived at Phoenix Sky Harbor airport on . . . can you believe it . . . *Easter morning.*

ONE-SIDED, UNCONDITIONAL LOVE

Nick is quiet, unnaturally self-controlled, while Natasha bursts with personality and energy. In the first couple months, though, whenever Nick thought Natasha was misbehaving, he would say something sternly in Russian that made her freeze with fear. My brother and his wife didn't know what to make of it, and eventually it happened frequently enough for them to ask an interpreter what was going on.

"What are you saying to your sister when she misbehaves?" the interpreter asked Nicholas in Russian.

Showing no emotion, Nick answered, "I'm telling her that if she doesn't stop, they will send us back to the orphanage."

After long silence David said, "Tell them this: Nicholas and Natasha, there is nothing either of you can ever do that will cause your new mother and me to send you back to the orphanage."

Love like you can't imagine.

LONG-SUFFERING LOVE

The last two years for David and Tonya have been a wild ride, like bungee jumping. Up and down. *Way* up and *way* down. And then down some more. Nick and Natasha, as you might suspect, brought with them uncommon challenges, so like all good relatives, some of us decided we would, well, help. And give unwelcomed advice.

Last fall the peace of our extended family blew up. For families who've undergone severe abuse, physical violence, and even death, our feud might have seemed like a pillow fight, but for us, it was as bad as it gets. Remarkably—and providentially—I was out of town. As the oldest brother, I'm usually in the middle of everything, often the *cause* of the problem.

Back to what David told me was the worst day of his life: I knew he and Tonya had been upset, even deeply offended, but it wasn't until he sent me an eight-page email last month that I realized how far he'd drifted from the family. He wrote passionately, angrily about an incident involving our other brother, Tom, who lives next door to them. (I live an hour away.) David and Tom had spoken very little in months, though I didn't know that beforehand. But we all knew there was a problem when Tom and Monica's two sons graduated from college on consecutive nights, and David and Tonya never showed up for the party.

A dreadful family-bashing incident had happened in Tom's home. You see, after the adoption, Nick had been diagnosed with reactive attachment disorder (RAD), stemming from a severe childhood in which he had suffered profoundly and become inwardly deadened, unable to bond with other people. In order to handle this, David was under doctor's orders to be very stern with Nick.

My mother, over time, had observed this and identified it as cruelty that bordered on abuse. She not only confronted David at a birthday party in Tom's home, she also brought others into it. Tom is reserved and soft-spoken, but what he thought of as his neutrality in this conflict was perceived by David (an up-front guy) as taking sides against him, even believing that the entire family was questioning, even undermining their parenting.

I appealed to David to forgive Tom, assuring him that Tom was his ally, noting that neither Tom nor Monica had followed up that incident with negative remarks, but David persisted. He was particularly angry that Tom hadn't apologized to him.

Waiting for Tom to make the first move, David was stuck in

unforgiveness. And Tom was just plain stuck. The "family explosion" had blown him away too, and he simply didn't know what to say. So nobody said anything and imagined everything.

ALL IN GOD'S PERFECT PLAN

Then an important memory surfaced in me.

While speaking with David about his pain, I suddenly remembered one of the worst days of *my* life. It was, perhaps, our *second-worst* family feud. At that time I was furiously angry about something *David* had done, something that had involved my children. In fact, I can't remember ever being angrier with anyone in my family. I told Dave then that he had *really* offended me!

Did he understand?

Are you kidding? He reacted!

Which only made me angrier. And then he dragged our mother into the middle of it. Before it was over, my grown children were crying.

And David *never apologized.*

To make matters worse, all of this climaxed on a Saturday, and my sermon that night (we have a Saturday evening church service) was about how to manage anger. Yeah, right! I was going to share God's Word on anger on a day I was blowing up like something in a Schwarzenegger flick.

That night, though, I began my message by confessing my sin . . . and how utterly unfit I was to talk about anger. I had everyone's attention as I plowed through my outline. At the end of the service we served the Lord's Table, and as I ate the bread and drank from the cup, as I stepped out of my world, out of my pain into the reality of Jesus, a miracle happened within me: Remembering how Jesus forgave me unconditionally, I determined to forgive my brother.

A PEACE OFFERING

So as we were talking about David's anger toward Tom, I asked him if he remembered the earlier feud between us. He did, but he had no recollection of why he was angry with me, and he certainly couldn't remember why I'd been angry with him.

"Know why you can't remember, Dave?"

"No," he said quietly.

"You can't remember because I asked *you* for forgiveness. I took the initiative. I even sent you a peace card with a wad of money, and I didn't ask for anything in return, not even for you to say you were sorry too. I took full responsibility for my side of the problem, and I let your side go. I let *you* go. Remember what I sent you?"

"Yeah," he answered meekly.

"Well, Dave, you never said you were sorry, but now I'm really glad that happened, because now I can appeal to you to take the high road in your relationship with Tom, to forgive him first, to initiate conversation with him. To put this behind you."

> [Jesus] himself is our peace, who has made the two one and has destroyed the barrier, the dividing wall of hostility . . . *through the cross,* by which he put to death their hostility.
> —Ephesians 2:14, 16

David was silent for a moment. He's a reasonable, godly man, and I knew he was hearing his big brother. "*Thank you,*" he said with feeling. "I'm going over to talk with Tom tomorrow." By the end of the next day eight months of misunderstanding and estrangement had melted in the warmth of God's love.

When David went next door to make peace with Tom, he probably didn't think about it this way, but he was carrying his cross. When Jesus took up his cross and died, he did it to reconcile us to the Father: "He humbled himself," the Bible says, "and became obedient to death—even death on a cross!"[2] Just a few verses earlier, the apostle Paul writes,

> Do nothing out of selfish ambition or vain conceit, but in humility consider others better than yourselves. Each of you should look not only to your own interests, but also to the interests of others. Your attitude should be the same as that of Christ Jesus.
>
> PHILIPPIANS 2:3–5

In other words, because Jesus laid down his life for us, we ought to lay down our lives for one another.[3] Because Jesus reconciled us to

God, we should make every effort to reconcile with others . . . which can be indescribably painful . . . like being crucified. Most Christians, it seems, are very clear on the first part—that Christ died for our sins—but don't seem so clear on the second part, which is that as we follow Christ we must take up our own cross.[4] The Cross not only brings us forgiveness for our sins and eternal life, *it changes everything*.

PASSION FOR THE CROSS

The cross of Christ is my passion. As we experience its power, it not only changes our relationship with God, it changes us. The Cross is God's offer of salvation *and wholeness*. Furthermore, the Cross is more than a principle, a concept. Certainly the Cross is truth, and there's truth in the message of the Cross, but the work of Christ is also a point of encounter, a front door into another reality. (Check out the cover of this book!)

> The message of the Cross is an intersection with the God of eternity.

Taking up your cross is transformational, because there is inherent power in the Cross. So often, it seems to me, the power of God for so many Christ-followers is an idea to be discussed, defined, understood—not a radically different dimension of life to be experienced in all its splendor and force. Becoming a Christian is a full immersion into a new life. The message of the Cross is an intersection with the God of eternity; living the Cross literally opens a way into another world, allowing the fresh wind of paradise to blow into us. When God sees us living like his Son, he favors us, fills us, and transforms us.

Ever open a window in your stuffy house and feel an exhilarating gust of cool spring air . . . perhaps bearing the fragrance of your neighbor's roses? Or how about when a summer breeze carries the pungent scent of fresh rain falling nearby? Take a deep breath! Then look again at the cover of this book and imagine feeling the Spirit's wind blowing right out of God's presence into your empty, colorless moments, perhaps your colorless life.

The Cross is the source of the life you've always wanted, a powerline directly from God to us. Living under the Cross, carrying ours daily, walking in complete submission to the Father, like Jesus did, turns on that power. When we take up our cross, when we die to self; when we live like Christ, something profoundly real happens in the spiritual dimension. Heaven comes down and fills our world with the presence and blessing of God.

Jesus prayed, "Thy kingdom come, Thy will be done on earth, as it is in heaven."⁵ When my brother Dave went next door to make things right with my other brother Tom, the Lord's Prayer was answered.

HEAVEN'S GATE

In this book we're going to look at the Cross from three sides.

First, we will see how the Cross takes us into a radically different reality. In other words, as I've already indicated, the Cross is a point of encounter with the presence of God, a point of escape from the seducing illusions of our dying world and a point of access into the power of God's kingdom. Part One shows us that the Cross is heaven's gate.

Second, we will reflect on the purposes of the Cross, that is, why Christ died and what that means practically for you and me. There are, of course, *many* reasons why Christ died—His work on the Cross was comprehensive—but we will be centering on what I consider to be the seven principal reasons why the Savior gave his life. Part Two is designed to be a journey of encounter at each of the Cross's major purposes.

Third, in the closing chapters, I will lead you into a commitment to the way of the Cross. Part Three will allow this book to end much like it begins, with a call to practice the presence of the Cross, to follow Christ by taking up your cross daily. To submit to God. To humble yourself. To love. To forgive. To discover that when you experience the Cross's power, everything in your life will change.

Are you ready for more of God?

It's time for your life to interface with a new reality!

To escape the matrix.

Let the journey begin. . . .

CHAPTER TWO

Reality:
Looking for a Phone Booth

You're here because you know something. What you know you can't explain. But you feel it. You've felt it your entire life. That there's something wrong with the world. You don't know what it is but it's there, like a splinter in your mind driving you mad.
—Morpheus, to Neo in *The Matrix*

Crawling in my skin
these wounds they will not heal
fear is how I fall
confusing what is real
—Linkin Park, "Crawling"

I loved *The Matrix*.
You know, the movie about . . . well . . . I wasn't so sure.
I confess, I had to see it with my eighteen-year-old son, Matt,

sitting next to me in the theater and unhappily hissing two- and three-word answers to my clueless questions. Actually, it was his second viewing, so I'm not convinced he initially grasped its meaning without someone helping him too.

Recently Matt was home for the holidays, and we watched it again, this time with "older friends" who said they'd seen the film a couple of years earlier and didn't get it. They needed someone to help them through it too, and this time I pretended to be the expert. As Will Rogers said, "An ignorant person is someone who doesn't know what you have just found out."

"Everything you're seeing right now," I told them at the beginning, "is 'the Matrix,' a computer program, virtual reality. Nothing you see in the huge city in the opening scenes is real, even though it *looks* real . . . and everyone you see thinks it's real . . . *believes* it's real."

Everybody except "the one," Neo, a hacker who suspects something is wrong with his world but can't begin to imagine what it might be. In an elaborately arranged secret meeting, Neo finally meets the mysterious Morpheus, a shadowy superman who seems to know Neo better than he knows himself. Morpheus offers Neo a life-choice: menacingly, he reaches out with his huge ebony fists, a large capsule in each . . . one blue . . . one red. "You take the blue pill," he says slowly, deliberately, "and the story ends. Take the red one, and you discover who you really are."

With hesitation, Neo reaches for the red pill. And swallows it. A moment later, Neo is shaking violently as if being electrocuted. The red pill catapults him into another world. Into the brutal truth that life as he knows it is nothing more than a massive computer-generated dream. The Matrix, his "real world," turns out to be a mega-illusion.

It probably sounds beyond goofy if you haven't seen the film, but in reality Neo's body is a battery, a human power source for artificial intelligence (AI). He's enslaved in suspended animation in a vast cavern of myriad other humans, their brains attached to a labyrinthine network of interface cables enabling them to provide electrical energy for AI—and to live together in the grand illusion of the Matrix.

BLASTING ALIENS

All of this is not entirely unlike my son Matt's own alternative world. Summers and Christmas vacations, when he's home from college, he carries his PC over to a friend's apartment. There, in the furniture-less living room, are folding tables littered with other PCs, all interconnected so as many as five or six people can play a single video game. Together they leave their real world and enter a network of electronic reality, a matrix. Except for an occasional hoot when someone disintegrates a digital alien, no one talks with anyone about anything else. Everyone's relationship with everyone else in the room is through the matrix.

> This is the world that you know. The world as it was at the end of the twentieth century. It exists now only as part of a neural-interactive simulation that we call the Matrix.
> —Morpheus

Matt has never actually lived inside a computer, but like Neo, his brain has. The advancing "reality" of video games is so amazing that he and his friends sit spellbound (his mother would say "enslaved") for hours—sometimes all night. "It's *so real,* Dad!" I've heard him exclaim.

I'm in computer-game preschool. I still like Atari and Game Boy, and I especially enjoy Tetris, where the little blocks fall out of the top of the screen. I've been totally absorbed into movies, though, like *The Matrix.* Or *Saving Private Ryan.* I relived the trauma of World War II for weeks after seeing that Spielberg masterpiece. I still think it should have won Best Picture, but I admit I'm partial to war films.

At the end of *Private Ryan,* if you're not crying, your brain is frozen in 1944. As the final credits roll up the black screen, you rise slowly in the dark and stumble toward the glowing red exit sign above the door. Then suddenly, surreally, you're back in your world: from a surround-sound firefight to the crowded restroom, through the buzzing lobby and out into the colorless, gritty parking lot.

A moment ago you were bleeding with Tom Hanks (Captain Miller); now you're walking among a throng of strangers. You've all been sitting in the same theater, sharing the same illusion, experiencing the same wonder, but you know only the two people who came with you. "What did you think?" you ask, as you and your friends readjust mentally and emotionally to the real world.

When I picked up a book on the making of *Private Ryan,* I discovered that the massive set had false-front French buildings and a river that doesn't run through it: the "river" ends just a few meters on either side of the village. I knew it was "only a movie," but I still couldn't believe it. It *seemed* so real.

I guess the parking lot is real.

What in the world is real? Is the world real?
What's real to you? Is it really real?

Some people like to speak in terms of redefining your reality. Personally, I believe reality is not so much a matter of definition or redefinition but of discovery and rediscovery. For the follower of Christ, the Cross is a doorway, an exit from the illusion of everything that appears utterly real. The Cross is a phone booth in the Matrix. (If you haven't seen the film, the heroes enter in and out of the Matrix by using a telephone.)[1] The Cross is an encounter with God and his world, a bridge across the flooded, impassable Jordan River into the Promised Land that flows with milk and honey.[2] If there's a door to heaven, the Cross is the key.

At the same time the Cross encounters *us*, confronts our failures and shame, our emptiness and need for God, our uncertain future, our self-absorbed individualism and self-destructive self-interest. The Cross is an entry point into another world, another dimension, a reality of ultimate freedom. The Cross is God's way out of a theater of fantasy, a celluloid world in which I only imagine I'm living.

> The Cross is an encounter with God and his world, a bridge across the flooded, impassable Jordan River into the Promised Land that flows with milk and honey.

JOURNEY

Some say there are many roads leading to God, but Jesus affirmed, "I am *the* way and *the* truth and *the* life."[3] Perhaps we could capture more fully the significance of this statement by looking at each of the three things Jesus calls himself.

First, Jesus is the road[4] to God. Interestingly, in this text, Jesus does not refer to himself as a door to God (more on that in a moment) but as a pathway to God. This suggests a journey, a way of life. In his *Following of Christ,* Thomas à Kempis calls this "the Royal Road of the Holy Cross." Certainly every road has a destination, but until you reach the specific place you're going, what matters most is how you travel—unwavering forward movement, staying focused, keeping perspective.

For the person who meets Christ, everything changes and nothing changes. In one sense, everything stays the same. Same house, same furniture. Same relationships, same job. On the other hand, how you understand the ordinary and daily routines of life changes dramatically. Every day becomes God's day, and every moment is a sacrament.

The writer of Hebrews tells us about this journey:

> Therefore, since we are surrounded by such a great cloud of witnesses, let us throw off everything that hinders and the sin that so easily entangles, and let us run with perseverance the race marked out for us. Let us fix our eyes on Jesus, the author and perfecter of our faith, who for the joy set before him endured the cross, scorning its shame, and sat down at the right hand of the throne of God. Consider him who endured such opposition from sinful men, so that you will not grow weary and lose heart.
>
> HEBREWS 12:1–3

Jesus, who walked the roads of life and finished his journey well, offers himself to us as *the* road of life, the way through life. He is *the* pathway to God and God-life, but he is also the doorway,[5] the entry point into a new reality, and *the Cross is an encounter with God and his world.*

Yes, I believe that Christ's death and resurrection are historical events. Paul was convinced of this as well, because he not only had a powerful personal encounter with the risen Christ,[6] he was also able to speak with dozens of actual eyewitnesses of those events.[7] Many have said that Paul's remarkable conversion is one of the most powerful indicators of the credibility of the Christian faith.

Yes, I believe that faith in Christ means getting the gospel right. True followers of Jesus are concerned about correct doctrine,[8] and for centuries Christians have labored to understand the precise meanings of Scripture. That Jesus died for my sins is an indisputable proposition, an absolute truth, the factual anchor of my faith.[9]

We will see throughout this book, though, that believing in Christ and taking up your cross is a journey of experience and encounter as well. Quoting the Old Testament, Jesus said, "Love the Lord your God with all your *heart* and with all your *soul* and with all your *mind*."[10] There is a mental element to our faith, but there's so much more.

Paul wrote, "My message and my preaching were not with wise and persuasive words, but with a demonstration of the Spirit's power, so that your faith might not rest on men's wisdom, but on God's power."[11] Eugene Peterson's *The Message* paraphrases the last part this way: "Your life of faith is a response to God's power, not to some fancy mental or emotional footwork by me or anyone else."

THE TRUTH

So Jesus is the pathway to God, a journey of daily encounters. *Second, Jesus is the truth.* There is perhaps no more controversial word: *truth.* Two thousand years ago Pilate asked, "What is truth?"[12] It's still the question *du jour,* although people are asking it a little differently.

Look carefully at Neo's response when Morpheus tells him that his world has blinded him to the truth: "What truth?" Not what *is* truth, which implies there might be an answer, but *what* truth, suggesting that any number of responses might work. National research by the Barna Group tells us that the great majority of Americans, and almost everybody born after 1970, believes that absolute truth is a thing of the past.[13] Allegedly, truth can't be known, and we hear it all the time: "What's true for you may not be true for me."

We're beginning to see the sunshine of our civilization sink into a dark sea of moral chaos, from Columbine to Enron. Earlier this year my son David Kinnaman, vice-president and strategic leader for the Barna Group, found an appalling absence of conscience among both nonreligious and religious young people: "Fewer than 1 in 10 teen-agers believes that music piracy is morally wrong."[14]

Relativism, though, is relatively foreign to the rest of the world. Lamin Sanneh, a native of Gambia and professor of Mission and World Christianity at Yale, writes,

The West, viewed broadly as a cultural system of ethics, images, music, literature as well as science and technology, has reduced the mystery of God to a cultural filibuster. [The West holds that] truth cannot be known with certainty, and one can be certain of that.[15]

Sociologist Alan Wolfe has written an entire book about this phenomenon, that American society is the first in human history to believe there is no such thing as objective, absolute truth.[16] Wolfe shows how, carried to its logical conclusions, the belief that there are no moral absolutes is philosophically indefensible. Though Wolfe cites a number of peculiar (and often bizarre) consequences of living in a truth vacuum, like any good American he makes no judgment about what's right or wrong with this kind of world, concluding that the jury is out and only time will tell if our society can survive.[17]

Christian leaders continue to argue for "the truth," correctness of belief in a world that simply doesn't care. Because so many people believe truth is relative, religious appeals based on truth can seem irrelevant. Worse yet, we live in a culture of contradiction, where people are increasingly intolerant of intolerance. Most of our social indicators, everything from teen suicide to divorce to prison population,[18] are shouting that we are a rudderless ship in a perfect storm.

Centuries ago the Hebrew prophet Hosea identified the primary cause of social disorder:

> [Because there is] no acknowledgment of God in the land . . . there is no faithfulness, no love. . . . There is only cursing, lying and murder, stealing and adultery; they break all bounds, and bloodshed follows bloodshed. Because of this the land mourns, and all who live in it waste away.[19]

RETHINKING TRUTH

The polarized lines are drawn. Is there an answer? Can we know with certainty that some things are true and some are not? Is there hope? Certainly not in the rhetoric of the right or the left, both of whom are convinced they're right (even though the left cannot be *absolutely* right).

Instead, our hope is in the person of Jesus Christ, who is *the source of abundant life* on the pathway to truth. But hold on to your hats, "this ride is going to take a sudden turn. Buckle your seat belt, Dorothy, because Kansas is going bye-bye."[20] When Jesus describes himself as the truth, we world-minded, rational-thinking Westerners jump straight to the linear conclusion that he means something like math. Or doctrine. Or religious correctness. Well, he did and he didn't.[21]

Jesus was full of truth,[22] but the richer meaning of the Greek term for "truth," *alétheia,*[23] is startling and can free us from our obsessive-compulsive need to make our point. *Alétheia* (and its family of derivative words) doesn't exactly mean "true" in the sense of "mathematically correct," or like a true/false exam. It carries a broader meaning as expressed by the following ideas: "truthfulness, dependability, righteousness, honesty, genuineness, authentic, the real deal." *Alétheia* is "reality as opposed to mere appearance."[24]

This is precisely the way John uses this term when Jesus calls himself "the true light," "the true bread," "the true vine," and when he calls his Father "the true God."[25] Jesus is the *real* light, the *real* bread, the *real* vine, and the God of the Bible is the *real* God. In John,[26] Jesus tells a Samaritan woman that the heavenly Father is looking for "real worshipers," that is, "those whose religious exercises are in actual fact and reality an approach to God, and not a shadowy ritual which either counterfeits or at best merely symbolizes the approach to God."[27]

Thus, in the following quotations from John's writings, wherever the word *truth* is used, read the verse using the phrase *true reality*:[28]

- Sanctify them by the *true reality;* your word (*logos*) is *true reality.*[29]

- *Real* worshipers must worship in spirit and in *true reality.*[30]

- Then you will know the *true reality,* and the *true reality* will set you free.[31]

- If we claim to have fellowship with him yet walk in the darkness, we lie and do not live by (in, according to) *true reality.*[32]

- If we claim to be without sin, we deceive ourselves and the *true reality* is not in us.[33]

- Pilate: "What is *truly real*?"[34]

- "I am the way and *the true reality* and the life."[35]

What does all this mean? In my view, people in our world aren't just searching for the right religious answers; *people are desperate for ultimate reality.* I've heard it, I've sung it: "Jesus is the answer for the world today." I'll no doubt sing it again, but when you think about it, "the answer" is so impersonal, so academic! Jesus the Son of God isn't *just* empirical, scientifically verifiable truth to which we give mental assent. No, Jesus is *personal reality,* the pathway, "the ultimate reality of the universe."[36] Jesus is a real person I can know, encounter, experience, and obey.

Jesus, the Word of God, is not some*thing* to which we give intellectual agreement, but some*one* whom we fully accept. Jesus is the real God made real flesh. When we are born again, his nature becomes our nature, his DNA becomes our DNA, his life reality becomes our reality. When we encounter Christ, *the* reality, our reality changes forever.

Partaking of Jesus is . . . well . . . like swallowing the red pill in *The Matrix.* Does this offend you?

> "I tell you the truth, unless you eat the flesh of the Son of
> Man and drink his blood, you have no life in you. Whoever
> eats my flesh and drinks my blood has eternal life, and I will
> raise him up at the last day. For my flesh is real food and my
> blood is real drink. Whoever eats my flesh and drinks my
> blood remains in me, and I in him." . . .
>
> On hearing [this], many of his disciples said, "This is a
> hard teaching. Who can accept it?"
>
> Aware that his disciples were grumbling about this, Jesus
> said to them, *"Does this offend you?"*
>
> JOHN 6:53–56, 60–61, EMPHASIS MINE

Consider a reality check next time you participate in the Lord's Supper. Let the body and blood of Christ take you out of the illusion of your transitory world and into the eternal realities of his kingdom.

REAL REALITY

Below is a list of extraordinary biblical statements about real reality. As you read them, ask yourself a few questions: Who's living an illusion, people who believe in Christ or people who don't? Who needs to take the red pill? Who needs to be washed in the blood of Jesus? What happens to people when they live in the wrong "reality"?

And *please,* pray as you read these verses. I don't merely want you to understand what I'm writing; I want you to encounter the Christ about whom I'm writing. My prayer is for you to enter his reality. Don't settle for "Wow, this is great stuff—interesting book." I want you to connect with the Jesus who has miraculously changed my reality and transformed my life.

The Bible on reality:

The god of this age has blinded the minds of unbelievers, so that they cannot see the light of the gospel of the glory of Christ, who is the image of God.

2 Corinthians 4:4

I tell you this, and insist on it in the Lord, that you must no longer live as the Gentiles do, in the futility of their thinking. They are darkened in their understanding and separated from the life of God because of the ignorance that is in them due to the hardening of their hearts. Having lost all sensitivity, they have given themselves over to sensuality so as to indulge in every kind of impurity, with a continual lust for more.

Ephesians 4:17–19

As I have often told you before and now say again even with tears, many live as enemies of the cross of Christ. Their destiny is destruction, their god is their stomach, and their glory is in their shame. Their mind is on earthly things. But our citizenship is in heaven. And we eagerly await a Savior from there, the Lord Jesus Christ.

Philippians 3:18–20

Therefore we do not lose heart. Though outwardly we are wasting away, yet inwardly we are being renewed day by day. For our light and momentary troubles are achieving for us an eternal glory that far outweighs them all. So we fix our eyes not on what is seen, but on what is unseen. For what is seen is temporary, but what is unseen is eternal.

2 CORINTHIANS 4:16–18

What I mean, brothers, is that the time is short. From now on those who have wives should live as if they had none; those who mourn, as if they did not; those who are happy, as if they were not; those who buy something, as if it were not theirs to keep; those who use the things of the world, as if not engrossed in them. For this world in its present form is passing away.

1 CORINTHIANS 7:29–31

Faith is being sure of what we hope for and certain of what we do not see.

HEBREWS 11:1

Ah yes, *faith*! We have to talk about faith in all this; after all, it's "the evidence of things not seen,"[37] and "we live by faith, not by sight."[38] This means that faith allows us to tap into reality . . . God's reality . . . the only true reality. Furthermore, faith is active, not passive. It's creative. It's transformational. *Faith is how we change our reality.* Let me explain.

BELIEVING "INTO"

Throughout the gospel of John, we come across a remarkable phrase found nowhere else in ancient Greek literature, a unique grammatical construction that means, literally, "believe *into*,"[39] in contrast with "believe *in*."[40] John had to invent (as it were) a new phrase to express fully this idea of faith.[41]

Instead of a weaker "I believe" or "I agree," New Testament faith is more like "I fully buy into it, and I'm going to let *God's* reality become *my* reality." To put it simply, we believe *in* an idea, but we must believe *into* Christ to encounter and experience reality. Look again at these familiar sayings:

> God so loved the world that he gave his one and only Son, that whoever believes in him [literally, "believes *into* him"] *shall not perish but have eternal life.*

> JOHN 3:16, EMPHASIS MINE

Faith is how we change our reality.

> To all who received him, to those who believed in his name [that is, "into *his name*"] *he gave the right to become children of God.*

> JOHN 1:12, EMPHASIS MINE[42]

Faith is a plunge into the real. Faith changes our reality by allowing us to look at what cannot be seen. As we think about the power of faith, however, I want to make something very clear: For the Christian, faith is not some cosmic power equally accessible to all living beings, some force I can use to bend spoon handles this way and my future that way.

Biblical faith is antithetical to the popular New Age idea that faith is power to reach your dreams. If you just visualize it . . . if you just say it . . . *no,* the object of our faith is the person of Christ alone, his word, his reality. Faith is not believing for what I want but living my life as though everything God says in his Word is *alétheia: the* truth, *the* ultimate reality. Faith has no intrinsic power, but Jesus does! Faith opens our hearts to heaven, opens heaven to our hearts, and releases the supernatural power of God into our world.

CAN YOU SEE?

A wonderful example is the ancient Israelite leader Joshua. His mentor, Moses, was the man God used to lead the chosen nation of Israel out of slavery in Egypt, through the Red Sea, and to the maroon shadows of Mount Sinai. After receiving the Ten Commandments and the rest of the Law there, the massive Israelite column snaked its way across the desert toward the Promised Land.

As is commonly known, that part of the world is neither scenic nor hospitable, and many of the people became disgruntled. Again and again Moses heard them whining in the backseat, "When are we going to get there?" At long last they reached the banks of the Jordan River, the eastern boundary of the Promised Land. When they imagined, though, that the people inhabiting their land had weapons of mass destruction, their collective faith in God's promise imploded in a wimpy gasp. I have a mental picture: To God, this moment looked and sounded like what happens when you let go of a big balloon. Sputtering erratically through the room, it shrinks in seconds from the size of a watermelon to a colored fragment puddled motionless on the floor.

Standing there at the Jordan, the faithlessness of the Israelites grew so fierce that the Lord couldn't contain his wrath. "Forty years," blared God's judgment: "Forty years you will wander in the desert, until every last one of you dies. Including you, Moses. But not Joshua and Caleb, because they have faith."[43]

Decades later all the original wanderers were resting in their sandy graves as their children and grandchildren returned to the banks of the Jordan. Straining his aging voice, Joshua said to the Israelites,

Come here and listen to the words of the LORD your God. This is how you will know that the living God is among you and that he will certainly drive out before you the Canaanites. . . . *See,* the ark of the covenant of the Lord of all the earth will go into the Jordan ahead of you.

JOSHUA 3:9–11, EMPHASIS MINE

Let's stop here for a moment with them. Let's see what they're seeing. Forty years before, their fathers and mothers had failed to enter the Promised Land for one principal reason: lack of faith.[44] The prospect and potential consequences of war with the various Canaanite peoples was more real to them than what God had promised. As a result, they failed to live in God's reality and enter Canaan; instead of a land flowing with milk and honey, they chose suffering and death in the wilderness of their own self-destructive choices.

Now at last a new generation was facing the same challenges: *to believe God or to believe their fears.* This time, though, the danger was not the giant Canaanite warriors and their well-defended cities. On this particular day, the Jordan River was a flood.

I've seen it, both the Jordan *and* desert floods. Here in Phoenix, my home city, we have a river (the Salt) that's nearly always desert-dry. I drive through the boulder-strewn, quarter-mile-wide gully several times a month. However, a couple decades ago we had record rains, and that dusty channel roared with the equivalent of one third the flow of the Mississippi River! All but one bridge toppled into the swirling chocolate flood, and for weeks we had a traffic nightmare.

You had to see it to believe it . . . and so did the Israelites. Looking at the flooded Jordan, they had to "see" God's promise. Remember, faith is the evidence of things not seen. Looking at one thing, they had to see another. I said this earlier: *Faith is how we change our reality.* Again, to qualify, faith is not how we *create* reality—faith is not the force. Faith is how we *transform*

> You do not know what you see, you see what you know.
>
> —H. R. Rookmaaker

our reality by identifying ourselves with God's reality. As the Israelites stood there, they faced a choice of realities: their "real" world or God's true reality; the flood or God's power to get them through the flood. This time, unlike their fathers and mothers, they made the right choice; this time they proved God was *alétheia.* God was true. God was real.

Joshua instructed them,

> "Choose twelve men from the tribes of Israel, one from each tribe. And as soon as the priests who carry the ark of the LORD—the Lord of all the earth—set foot in the Jordan, its waters flowing downstream will be cut off and stand up in a heap."
>
> So when the people broke camp to cross the Jordan, the priests carrying the ark of the covenant went ahead of them. Now the Jordan is at flood stage all during harvest. Yet as soon as the priests who carried the ark reached the Jordan and their feet touched the water's edge [just like God said], the water from upstream stopped flowing.
>
> JOSHUA 3:12–16

[The water] piled up in a heap a great distance away, at a town called Adam in the vicinity of Zarethan, while the water flowing down to the Sea of the Arabah (the Salt Sea) was completely cut off. So the people crossed over opposite Jericho. The priests who carried the ark of the covenant of the LORD stood firm on dry ground in the middle of the Jordan, while all Israel passed by until the whole nation had completed the crossing on dry ground.

JOSHUA 3:16–17

> Faith may be defined as an illogical belief in the occurrence of the improbable.
> —H. L. Mencken

Believing is seeing.
Can you see it?

JAHWEH JIREH

Let's revisit verses 10 and 11 for a moment:

This is how you will know that the living God is among you and that he will certainly drive out [your enemies]. *See,* the ark of the covenant of the Lord of all the earth will go into the Jordan ahead of you.

The Hebrew word for "see" is in the same word family as *Jahweh Jireh,* which means "the Lord *will provide,*" a phrase we find much earlier in the story of Abraham, when God mysteriously told him to sacrifice his only son.

Abraham, the father of the Jewish nation, took wood for the burnt offering and placed it on Isaac, and he himself carried the fire and the knife. As the two of them went on together, Isaac spoke up and said to Abraham, "Father?"

"Yes, my son?" Abraham replied.

"The fire and wood are here," Isaac said, "but where is the lamb for the burnt offering?"

Abraham answered, "*God himself will provide* [*Jahweh Jireh*] the lamb for the burnt offering, my son."[45]

And he did. When Abraham and Isaac reached the site of the sacrifice, there was a ram with its horns snagged in a thicket. The force of Abraham's faith didn't create the ram or drag it into the bush, but his faith did engage him in the reality of God's provision. For Christians, this narrative prefigures the death of God's only Son; Jahweh indeed provided a sacrifice, Jesus Christ. Some Bible scholars believe the place of Abraham's sacrifice[46] was the very spot where, one day, Jesus would die for our sins.

Somehow, in the mystery of the moment, Abraham actually "saw" this. Listen to what Jesus says (are you sitting down?):

> "Your father Abraham rejoiced at the thought of *seeing my day*; he *saw* it and was glad." [Seeing Christ transformed Abraham's reality!]
>
> "You are not yet fifty years old," the Jews said to him, "and you have seen Abraham!"
>
> "I tell you the truth," Jesus answered, "before Abraham was born, *I am!*"
>
> At this, they picked up stones to stone him.
>
> JOHN 8:56–59, EMPHASIS MINE

Why did the Jews react this way? Because in their minds what Jesus said was blasphemy. To them, he was identifying himself as Jahweh, the I AM, the holy God who appeared to Moses in the burning bush.[47]

Listen to how Eugene Peterson presents this passage in *The Message:*

> "Abraham—your 'father'—with jubilant faith *looked down the corridors of history* and saw my day coming. He saw it and cheered."[48]
>
> The Jews said, "You're not even fifty years old—and Abraham saw you?"
>
> "Believe me," said Jesus, "*I am who I am* long before Abraham was anything."
>
> That did it—pushed them over the edge. They picked up rocks to throw at him. But Jesus slipped away, getting out of the Temple.

Faith is a phone booth in the Matrix, an exit from the dead-end reality of time and space.[49] Faith "looks down the corridors of history." Close your eyes and imagine this: silver-haired Abraham—

maybe he looked a little like Gandalf in *Lord of the Rings*—flying at warp speed through a tunnel of time. It's like he's in a five-star sci-fi film with outrageous sound and special effects. Can't you just hear the whooshing and whining and whirring as Abraham's faith rockets him through "the corridors of history" into the future?

> Unfortunately, no one can be told what the Matrix is. You have to see it for yourself.
> —Morpheus
>
> Believers see a sign. Unbelievers see nothing.
> —Dietrich Bonhoeffer

Think for a moment about the unique relationship among these words: *faith*, *seeing*, and *provision*. What does it mean that God provides, that God *pro-vides*? This familiar English word is derived from a Latin root that means, literally, "to see in advance"! (In other words: *pro-vision*, or *fore-sight*.) The Hebrew term *jireh* is a similar convergence of meaning: in the Abraham-Isaac narrative of Genesis, it's translated, "The LORD will *provide*," while in Joshua 3:11, the same root word reads, "*See!*"

Believing is seeing.

Faith sees.

By faith you see what you can't see, and faith releases the *pro-vision* (the vision ahead) of God for your future. For the believer, faith is reality.

"*See,* the ark of the covenant of the Lord of all the earth will go into the Jordan *ahead of you.*" The ark, the resting place of the radiant cloud of God's glory, goes *ahead of us* into the floods of life. Because the radiant presence of Jesus goes before us into the mess of our circumstances, he can rightfully say to us about the future, "Been there, done that." It's incredible! God goes into the flooded river *first*. Can you see him there, waiting for you to enter his reality?

THE LIFE

Jesus is the pathway to wholeness, a journey of daily encounters with God. Jesus is the truth, that is, ultimate reality. *Jesus is the life*. Notice the perfect sequence:

Journey (Way), Reality (Truth), Wholeness (Life)

When we hold Christ's hand as we travel through life, we encounter and experience his reality—*the* reality. When Jesus is my way, my journey, he takes me into the reality of God and brings the reality of his kingdom into me. This is life, *abundant* life! The convergence of our journey with the way of Christ into the ultimate reality of God *is* life.

Jesus said, "I came so they can have *real* and eternal life, *more and better life than they ever dreamed of.*"[50] Not surprisingly, this is the great American dream: "*life, liberty, and the pursuit of happiness.*" What the fathers of our nation had in mind when they wrote this memorable phrase was most certainly not what most of us think regarding the pursuit of happiness in the twenty-first century![51] For us, it's become the restless quest for something (or some things) to give us a sense of wholeness and meaning. It's the age-old human search for significance, but we just "can't get no satisfaction." Not in wealth, health, sex, or success.

> Anything less than God will let you down. Anything less than God is not rooted in eternal reality. It has built-in failure.
> —E. Stanley Jones

When our life-focus drifts from God to anything else, when we devote ourselves to what *we* think will bring us happiness, we end up worshiping gods of our own making. It's idolatry, pure and simple. As we bow down, we discover painfully that our gods have no power to satisfy us, let alone heal us and make us whole. They do, however, have the power to control us, even to enslave us.

In contrast, listen to this extraordinary ancient promise: "[The LORD] will be the sure foundation for your times." In other words, you'll have a deep sense of peace and safety, no matter where the journey of life takes you, because the LORD will be "a rich store of salvation and wisdom and knowledge; the fear of the LORD is the key to this treasure."[52] Jesus echoes these words in the Sermon on the Mount:

> Do not worry, saying, "What shall we eat?" or "What shall we drink?" or "What shall we wear?" For the pagans run after all these things [the pursuit of happiness], and your heavenly Father knows that you need them. But seek first his kingdom

and his righteousness, and all these things will be given to you as well.

MATTHEW 6:31–33

> Why, then, are you afraid to take up your cross, which leads to the kingdom? In the Cross is salvation; in the Cross is life; in the Cross is protection from enemies. In the Cross is infusion of heavenly sweetness; in the Cross is strength of mind; in the Cross is joy of Spirit. In the Cross is height of virtue; in the Cross is perfection of sanctity. There is no . . . hope of eternal life, but in the Cross.
> —Thomas à Kempis[54]

Be assured that Jesus came so you "can have *real* and eternal life, *more and better life than you ever dreamed of.*"[53] Jesus is the way (the journey) *and* the truth (ultimate reality) *and* the life (wholeness) you've always wanted.

FOR REFLECTION AND DISCUSSION

What is your reality? What shapes how you think, how you feel, how you make decisions, how you live your life? In some ways, the realities of the Matrix are more appealing than the real world Neo discovers when he swallows the red pill. Read 1 Corinthians 3:18 and Hebrews 11:24–26. In light of what you've learned in this chapter, what aspects of your life are stuck in the matrix of time and space? Seek opportunities to discuss this with your family and friends.

CHAPTER THREE

The Cross 101

The only person who deserves to be called a theologian is the one who comprehends the visible and manifest things of God seen through suffering and the Cross.
—Martin Luther

The sea spray was biting cold, but it was a magnificent, cloudless day. Billowing sails danced around us in the glittering sunlight. Just ahead loomed the massive Golden Gate Bridge, arching north from misty San Francisco to the emerald hills of Marin County.

Curled up in the bow to shelter himself from the chilling wind, Matt refused to lift his head to look at the grand sight. "Matt," I yelled impatiently, "you have to see this!" Reluctantly he braved exposure for a few seconds, looked up, and mumbled something like "that's cool" as he quickly retreated below the side of the boat.

As for me, I wasn't going to miss this moment! Soaring skyward above us, the Golden Gate held special memories. My wife, Marilyn, and I had once driven across that bridge into our future. Years ago, we rambled up the California coast in our tiny Datsun pickup for our honeymoon camping trip. There in the distance, at the north end of the span, I could see the viewpoint where we'd stood close to each other for a first photo of our new life together.

I love bridges!

Stone arches across the Thames in London. The Pont Alexandre III over the Seine in Paris. Covered wooden spans framed by crimson foliage in Vermont. Glistening steel skeletons carrying railroads and families across the Mississippi into St. Louis and the American West. Miles and miles of Interstate across Lake Pontchartrain into the narrow streets of old New Orleans. The gorgeous rainbow of the Coronado Bridge arching perilously into the sky over mammoth naval vessels in San Diego's harbor.

I love bridges!

One of my favorites is in my own state of Arizona, across Glen Canyon, a breathtaking, deep purple chasm that widens into the Grand Canyon of the Colorado. Just below the huge dam at Lake Powell, the span over Glen Canyon is the second-highest steel-arch bridge in the world.[1]

Sooner or later you're going to have a bridge to cross. It might be an unnoticed culvert under a country road or, if you live in Oakland and work in San Francisco, the Bay Bridge. Some obstacles along the road of life are impassable without a bridge.

As we journey through this book about God's outrageous plan for a happy life, there are at least two bridges *everyone* must cross in order to live and finish well. The first is, without question, the most important: the bridge across the canyon of time and space into the presence and pleasure of God.

THE BRIDGE OF SALVATION [2]

No more weighty question faces us than this: Is there a God—a Supreme Being—and, if so, how *can* I, how *should* I relate to that Being? What place in my life is there for the divine, the supernatural?

Everyone knows there's more to life than just living and dying:

Human life has to be more than a chance collection of atoms and molecules. Just this week I heard pastor and bestselling author John MacArthur speaking about naturalistic assumptions. He'd heard a scientist, lecturing about the complexity of life, say that constructing a self-sustaining, self-repairing, self-reproducing machine is an engineering impossibility. Yet every living cell in the universe is encoded to be self-sustaining, self-repairing, and self-reproducing. Surely when we ponder the wonder of life's *physical* elements—especially the miracle of human life—we find ourselves compelled to ask questions about life's *spiritual* meaning.

"The heavens declare the glory of God," the psalmist wrote. "The skies proclaim the work of his hands. Day after day they pour forth speech; night after night they display knowledge."[3] Eugene Peterson brilliantly renders another Scripture, "Unspoken truth is spoken everywhere."[4]

Sooner or later, then, everyone gives truth a try. We can't help ourselves! Restlessly we search our own souls. Relentlessly we seek the divine, for we bear an insatiable sense that somewhere, on the other side of that deep canyon, is Someone who calls out to us for relationship. But how do we get from here to there?

CROSSING THE CHASM

I know this is really basic, but bridges connect two points over a hazardous or impassable canyon or body of water. However, what many don't know is that bridges are built from both ends at the same time and, in a marvel of structural engineering, meet precisely in the middle. Like the bridge I mentioned earlier, the perilous span over Glen Canyon.

Some years ago Marilyn and I spent time in the visitors' center there, which is perched perilously over the azure water foaming out of the dam's base hundreds of feet below. Especially unnerving are large black and white photo displays of the steel bridge under construction, the two ends, like bristles of silver toothpicks, growing out of the sheer sides of the massive gorge. In the middle, *nothingness*. A gaping gap. Anyone who stares at those pictures can imagine a construction worker inching his way to the edge of the abyss as he risks plummeting to the raging waters far below. It gives me vertigo just writing about it!

Years later those photos flashed back at me as I was preparing an Easter sermon. Right there in those stunning images is an illustration of how so many people think about religion. God is reaching out from his side of the canyon, but I have to work hard on mine, like the ancients of Babel who determined to build "a tower that reaches to the heavens."[5] They didn't get very far. In language ringing with ridicule, the Bible reports that "the LORD *came down* to see this city and the tower." Like one of us bending over an anthill, God had to stoop down to see what in the world those proud people were doing. Not much, he decided. In fact, what little they were doing was so self-driven he had to put an end to their foolishness.

Paul wrote famously, "All have sinned and *fall short* of the glory of God."[6] No one understood this better, as Paul had done everything humanly possible to build his own bridge to God:

> If anyone else thinks he has reasons to put confidence in the flesh, I have more: circumcised on the eighth day, of the people of Israel, of the tribe of Benjamin, a Hebrew of Hebrews; in regard to the law, a Pharisee; as for zeal, persecuting the church; as for legalistic righteousness, faultless.
>
> PHILIPPIANS 3:4–6

So when I begin to feel hopeless in my self-pursuit of God, I start thinking that maybe I'd rather live my life as if there were no God in heaven. And that's what many people do, because the human quest for God is more difficult than getting the space shuttle to Mars.

> Silence
> Trying to fathom the distance,
> Looking out 'cross the canyon carved
> By my hands.[7]

THE BRIDGE ACROSS TO GOD

Think about this: I can't even live up to my *own* expectations—New Year's resolutions rarely make it past mid-January! How then can

I fool myself into believing that somehow, maybe, I can live up to *God's* expectations for me? Yet every one of us has moments (sometimes these "moments" last for years) when we think we can actually do something to get God's attention or impress him in some way. This, in one form or another, is the central belief of *every* religion in the world *except Christianity.*

Every other religion in the world is essentially the same. Except the Christian faith, because every religion, at its core, expects human effort to reach out to a waiting God on the other side of a great divide. Perhaps that's why this saying is so popular: "God helps those who help themselves."[8] In other words, God may do a lot, but we have to do something too.

In bold contrast, the unique and extraordinary message of the gospel is that God took on the bridge-building business all by himself. In an engineering impossibility, he built the entire span from his side of the canyon to ours. This is the gospel truth, the "good news," that righteousness starts from God and comes to us, not the other way around: "In the gospel a *righteousness from God* is revealed, a righteousness that is by faith from first to last."[9]

The Bible has a special word for this act of God's unconditional love for us: *grace.* Grace isn't God meeting us halfway—if he did that, it wouldn't be grace. Halfway is conditional; grace is unconditional. Grace is God going the whole way, all the way. Grace isn't God's good help for everyone who does their best: grace is God's intervention in our helplessness.

> Since we've compiled this long and sorry record as sinners . . . and proved that we are utterly incapable of living the glorious lives God wills for us, God did it for us. Out of sheer generosity he put us in right standing with himself. A pure gift. He got us out of the mess we're in and restored us to where he always wanted us to be. And he did it by means of Jesus Christ. God sacrificed Jesus on the altar of the world to clear that world of sin.
>
> ROMANS 3:23–25 THE MESSAGE

I love bridges, *especially this one:* the Cross of Christ, the bridge across to God. Without the Cross before us, full and intimate relationship with God is impossible. For the believer, Jesus is "the way and the truth and the life," and "no one comes to the Father" except through him.[10] This is the exhilarating good news of the gospel. For the unbeliever, it's the offense of the Cross, the outrageous idea that we can do nothing—can't do anything—to earn God's favor, that cuts to the root of human pride.

> There's a bridge to cross the great divide;
>   a way was made to reach the other side.
> The mercy of the Father cost His Son His life.
>   His love is deep.
>   His love is wide.
> There's a cross to bridge the great divide.[11]

THE BRIDGE OVER TROUBLED WATERS

I grew up in a single-income family in the fifties, a family with a *small* single income. My dad was a high school woodshop teacher, and my mom devoted herself to her three boys. On dad's meager salary, they bought a car, a home, sparse furnishings—and orthodontia and a college education for each of us. To supplement my parents' support, as a college student, I worked for a huge furniture warehouse. It was hard, hot, menial work for minimum wage: loading sofas into station wagons and—the worst—*un*loading mattresses from eighteen-wheelers superheated by the scorching Arizona summer sun.

Even more unbearable, though, was my boss. A chain-smoker, the guy didn't have training in either human relations or anger management. He was a huge guy, too. One sweltering day when a customer's child had an "accident" in the financing office, I was the first slave he spotted. Pointing to the disgusting mass on the tile floor, he gruffly demanded, "Clean this up."

It was one of those moments in life when time stands still. Everything seemed to be unfolding in slow motion as I stared at the pile and considered my options. Surprising myself, I replied firmly, "Sorry, this is *not* my job." One look up into Goliath's red face and flashing eyes, though, and I knew I'd said the wrong thing. Whether or not it was officially my responsibility, I knew I was going to do it or I'd soon be working somewhere else.

So, gag me, I cleaned it up.

My boss, though, didn't forget my insubordination. He made my life miserable at every turn, until one day I determined to do something I'd learned in a Basic Youth Conflicts seminar taught by Bill Gothard. You've had those circumstances, haven't you, when something you heard in church or in a Bible study suddenly makes real-life sense?

I had learned—and wanted to forget—that I was to give up my rights and submit to people whom God placed in authority over me. So, with both conviction and uncertainty, I meekly approached my boss and asked him to forgive me for my arrogance and unwillingness to respect him.

His response was startling. I can't say his eyes flooded with tears, but I'll never forget the expression on his face as he replied sincerely, "I've never had something like this happen to me in my life. I accept your apology."

Did he change? No. Did I change? Yes. Did my act of obedience to God change my attitude? Yes. Literally, God's peace filled my soul. God took over when I let go, and I discovered the power and freedom of dying to myself. Taking up my cross took me into God-reality.

GOD'S OUTRAGEOUS PLAN

Every Christian believer, it seems, has at least a basic understanding of the *vertical* dimension of the Cross of Christ, that the work of Jesus on Calvary is a bridge to God. We Christians would also affirm that relationship with God without the Cross is impossible, for without the shedding of Christ's blood there is no forgiveness of sins.

My sin, oh, the bliss of this glorious thought!
My sin, not in part but the whole,
    is nailed to the cross, and I bear it no more,
Praise the Lord, praise the Lord, O my soul![12]

What believers often don't seem to understand is that the Cross of Christ has an equally powerful *horizontal* dimension. Just as *eternal* salvation can't happen without the Cross, *daily* salvation can't happen without it either.[13] The Cross is not only God's wonderful plan for your eternity, it's also his outrageous plan for a happy life, starting today. Believing in the sacrifice of Christ's life pays for our salvation, but taking up your cross,[14] that is, fully embracing the message of the Cross, will take you on an extraordinary journey of healing, wholeness, and extraordinary personal peace.

The Cross is an outrageous plan because, as Paul wrote, "The message of the cross is foolishness to those who are perishing, but to us who are being saved it is the power of God."[15] The Cross is not only our bridge to God, it's the bridge over the troubled waters of daily life.

Paul's first letter to the Christians in the Greek city of Corinth was written to people who had miserable relationships with one another. Life for them was painful, not peaceful, so Paul said this: "I resolved to know nothing while I was with you *except Jesus Christ and him crucified.*"[16] In effect, Paul is telling us that the nitty-gritty, practical solution to our relational conflicts is the power of the Cross. Paul calls it "God's secret wisdom."[17] I call it God's secret *weapon*! The low road is the high road.

The Cross bridges the chasm between humans and God. It's the Cross that heals my relationship with God, and it's the Cross that crucifies the power of selfishness and releases me to God-love[18] others. The Cross is God in Christ reaching down to me in love. The Cross is about Christ in me reaching out to love others the way God loves me.

You've probably heard people say, as they stretch their arms out wide, "Jesus loves you *this* much." That's precisely how Christ was nailed to the cross. But look! Look again at Jesus' hands! *They're* open wide too. So if you and I are having a conflict, as I take one of his nail-pierced hands and you take the other, Jesus becomes a bridge of healing and reconciliation between us.

Only the Cross can bring us together with God. Only the Cross can bring *us* together. Paul wrote about this intensely practical side of the Cross when he declared,

> He [Jesus] tore down the wall we used to keep each other at a distance. . . . Christ brought us together through his death on

the Cross. *The Cross got us to embrace,* and that was the end
of the hostility.

EPHESIANS 2:14, 16 THE MESSAGE, EMPHASIS MINE

A LITTLE CROSS GOES A LONG WAY

A year or so ago I was having lunch with a retired friend. Nearly
eighty, you'd think he was in his mid-sixties: after retiring from pas-
toral ministry in a large Lutheran church in California, he launched a
stewardship enrichment ministry that has helped churches and non-
profits raise hundreds of millions of dollars for Christian work. With
a huge grin and the enthusiasm of someone telling you how his daughter's volleyball team just won the state championship, Pastor K leaned
into my face to tell me about how one grumpy old man discovered
the power of the Cross.

Working with a local church to raise money for new construction,
Pastor K, at an initial meeting, told everyone that their journey
together was not going to be about money. Instead, he announced, it
would be about witness. Handing out dozens of little golden cross
lapel pins, he let it be known that *everyone* around the table would
make a commitment to sharing their faith. They could use their cross,
he explained, as a way to begin a conversation with others about Jesus.

Nearly every one in the room nodded their acceptance, some
reluctantly. One man, though, put his foot down: "I'm not going to
do that," he said gruffly. Yet somehow one of those little crosses ended
up in his pocket.

Now, most people in his church didn't know that he and his father
had had a terrible falling out. They hadn't spoken for years, and now
his dad was in the hospital. Dying. Overcome by guilt and regret, the
man determined he would visit his ailing father.

Not knowing if he would be shouted out of the hospital room, he
slipped uncertainly through the half-opened door. The two men
exchanged glances. Neither said a word. Nervously, the younger man
fumbled with something deep in his pocket—the little golden cross
from Pastor K. Inadvertently, he pulled it out and, speechless, held it
in his hand.

"What's that you have there?" his father asked.

"See for yourself. It's a cross."

As the fleck of bright metal flashed in the sunlight pouring through the window, the father began to cry. Reaching out to his son, he said softly, "It's time for us to heal this wound."

Openly weeping, they asked each other's forgiveness. Literally, in only a moment, the sight of that tiny cross—and the reminder of its message of love, forgiveness, and hope—changed two men, and everyone who loved them, forever.

Pastor K, now gripping my wrist tightly, finished the story. At the funeral, not many weeks later, the grateful son took that little cross and laid it on his father's still breast. *The Cross brought them to embrace,* and that was the end of their hostility.

THE EMBRACE OF THE CROSS

How does the Cross get us to embrace? Jesus laid down his life for me. When I lay down my life for him and others, when I give up my rights, my right to be right, when I crucify my hostility, when I die to myself, something extraordinary happens to me. Laying down my life sets me free from the power of "me." Listen to Jesus himself: "Anyone who does not take his cross and follow me is not worthy of me." But what does this mean, to take my cross? Jesus adds these words: "Whoever finds his life will lose it, and whoever loses his life for my sake will find it."[19] *This* is God's outrageous plan for a happy life! Here's how it reads in *The Message:*

If your first concern is to look after yourself, you'll never find yourself. But if you forget about yourself and look to me, you'll find both yourself and me.

In other words, meaning and wholeness come to us in a way that's fundamentally contradictory to popular wisdom. The pride in us and the self-possessed world around us says, "Watch out for number one. You have to do what's right for you. Blah, blah, blah." This is, perhaps, the greatest irony of the Christian life—that surrender to God, giving it up, letting go is the path to peace and fulfillment. Conversely, not surrendering to God, not giving it up, not letting go, is the path to pain and self-destruction. *It's in our best interest not to live for our best interests!*

According to one of the Beatitudes, the meek are blessed, "for they will inherit the earth."[20] The *Amplified Bible* explodes,

> Blessed (happy, blithesome, joyous, spiritually prosperous—
> with life-joy and satisfaction in God's favor and salvation,
> regardless of their outward conditions) are the meek (the
> mild, patient, long-suffering), for they shall inherit the earth!

So happy and prosperous are those who give it up, because they're the ones who, in the end, will get it all. Wow!

Or you can have this un-Beatitude: "Cursed are those who won't give it up, because in the end, they'll lose it all." Can't you just hear the screams of the self-absorbed people in your life? Can't you hear yourself protesting, "You mean I have to die to live?! That's madness!" No, that's the Cross: foolishness to the world, but God's outrageous plan for a happy life for those who believe. Jesus died to live, and Jesus died for you to live. To live like Jesus is to die to yourself. Protest if you wish, but this isn't just good advice for making the most of your life—it's the *only* way to make the most of your life. It's outrageous:

> I tell you the truth, unless a kernel of wheat falls to the
> ground and dies, it remains only a single seed. But if it dies,
> it produces many seeds. The man who loves his life will lose
> it, while the man who hates his life in this world will keep it
> for eternal life.
>
> JOHN 12:24–25

It's astonishing:

> Everyone who has left houses or brothers or sisters or father
> or mother or children or fields for my sake will receive a hun-
> dred times as much and will inherit eternal life. But many
> who are first will be last, and many who are last will be first.
>
> MATTHEW 19:29–30

GOD'S SECRET WEAPON

It's outrageous. Unthinkable. But it's true, and it works! Here's an extraordinary letter I received from someone in my church, *after* she heard me speak on the Cross as God's secret weapon.

> *Dear Pastor G:*
>
> *I felt compelled to thank you for last Saturday's sermon on the Cross. I have been having a very difficult time at work since January. Battle lines are drawn and sides taken. There are power struggles, backstabbing, and he said/she said matches in addition to deadline concerns and general personality conflicts. I've been losing sleep over work issues, finding myself very angry and resentful.*
>
> *I'd been struggling with the I-know-I'm-right and I'm-not gonna-back-down syndrome you described. Your sermon got me thinking otherwise, that is, "How am I going to use this stuff about the Cross at work?"*
>
> *Today I sucked it up, swallowed my pride, and apologized to a coworker because I've handled some situations inappropriately. We proceeded to have a good airing out, and some of the other tensions eased too. Today was the first good day in months. In my quest to do the right thing and not just be right, God rewarded me! He's comforted me, and my anger and resentment are gone (at least for today!). I've been praying for this to happen every day, but I needed the combination of prayer and your explanation of how to be obedient to His will to make the difference. A huge weight has been lifted.*
>
> *It's just past 11:00 p.m. I'm sleepy and I'm going to have a good night's sleep for a change. THANK YOU!*
>
> *Sincerely,*
> *Lisa*

This *is* foolishness to those who don't know God, but for believers it's "God's secret wisdom," God's secret weapon!

The Cross seems like sheer silliness to those hellbent on destruction, but for those on the way of salvation it makes perfect sense. This is the way God works, and most powerfully as it turns out. It's written, "I'll turn conventional wisdom on its head."

1 CORINTHIANS 1:18–19 THE MESSAGE

Have you heard this? Said this yourself?

> I have my feelings about this.
> I have to do what's right for me.
> I have to protect my rights.
> I have to think about myself in all this.

This kind of thinking is so widespread that, in contrast, the wisdom of God seems just plain dumb. The Cross, giving everything up because serving others is more important, means that "those who belong to Christ Jesus have nailed the passions and desires of their sinful nature to his cross and crucified them there."[21]

Pray this:

> *Heavenly Father, I thank you that you are not out there somewhere waiting for me to do something spiritual. You saw me on the other side of the canyon, helpless. So you built a bridge by sending your dear Son, Jesus, to become flesh and die on the cross for my sins. I believe it! You've done it all, and all I have to do is believe. And thank you, Jesus, that your death on the cross is an example to me of how it is more blessed to give than to receive. You didn't come to receive anything from me except my love in return for yours. You didn't come to be ministered to, but to minister, and to give your life as a payment for my sin. You laid down your life for your enemies . . . for me. I hear your voice calling me to let go, to give it up, to trust you. Show me how I can do this at home, at work, at church. I confess, Blessed are the meek, for they will inherit the earth. Amen.*

FOR REFLECTION AND DISCUSSION

In your view, are *both* you and God working on either end of the bridge? If so, why? Either way, consider rereading the Bible passages in the first part of this chapter, then pray that God will make his promises of unconditional grace utterly real in your heart and life.

Begin an "Outrageous Plan Journal" and maintain it for forty or fifty days. Give special attention to the Scripture verses in each section of this book. Make notes to yourself about the things in your life that cause you pain or stress—and how, specifically, the message of the Cross applies to each of those situations.

CHAPTER FOUR

The Passion Reloaded: More Blood Than a Mel Gibson Film

That greatest and most glorious of all subjects, the Cross of Christ.
   —John Stott

All that Christ was in heaven or on earth was put into what he did there. You don't understand Christ till you understand his cross.
   —P. T. Forsyth

The cross.

Christians love it. They love it for what Jesus did on it. They wear it. They want it on their church buildings. At Word of Grace, where I serve as senior minister, people have complained not a few times about the relative absence of the cross and other symbols inside our worship center. I remind them that we have a cross on the front of the podium that becomes huge when projected onto our 18' x 24' screen. But for some folks, that's not enough.

Outside our building, we have a tall steel cross prominently affixed near the gabled peak, high above the sanctuary entrance. Yet I can't tell you how many people have complained about *that* cross. "It's lovely," I reply. "It towers above everything else, right there where everyone can see it." It's even spotlighted at night!

But *that* cross bothers people! What's wrong with our exterior cross? It's not *exactly* in the middle! Our architect suggested it would look better if placed a little off-center, but for some believers, the cross should be in the precise middle of everything.

When I talked about our asymetrical cross in a recent sermon, one of our "deeper" members explained to me its richer meaning. Pointing above us, he asked me, "Can't you see it?"

I squinted into the bright blue sky. "See what?"

"See the point of the roof?" he continued. "It's like the throne of God. And there's the cross, at the right hand of the Father."

Um . . . okay.

A sweet thought, but just writing about it makes me chuckle. Maybe I'd "spiritualize" it this way: Our cross at Word of Grace is off-center because I'm offbeat. In any case . . .

Christians love the cross!

Conversely, many non-Christians despise it. Prominent scholar John Stott points out that Friedrich Nietzsche rejected Christianity for its "weakness," its belief in "God on the cross." Others have done so for its supposedly "barbaric" teachings. According to Stott, Oxford philosopher Sir Alfred Ayer, well known for his antipathy to Christianity, wrote that among religions of historical importance there is a strong case for considering Christianity the worst. Why? Because it rests on "the allied doctrines of original sin and vicarious atonement, which are intellectually contemptible and morally outrageous."[1]

As the principle symbol of the Christian faith, we want the cross featured conspicuously in our buildings, and we wear it with tenderness. But the fact that the cross was a form of gruesome excecution is lost in our fondness for "Christian" jewelry.

Imagine people wearing little silver and gold guillotines in joyful memory of the French Revolution. Why, we could make them authentic, razor sharp. And we could include multicolored, soft little plastic guys to wedge into the blade, neck first

Okay, Okay! I know I'm probably taking this too far, but history tells us that for this very reason, that is, the association of the cross with the execution of common criminals, early Christians avoided using the symbol in the first hundred years of the church. Look around at any large crowd of Christians today, though, and you'll see crosses of every imaginable design, including many with a tiny Jesus hanging there, dying.

A CROSS HISTORY

Most people know that crucifixion is among the cruelest forms of execution ever devised. The condemned man, before dying, could hang for days in excruciating pain. (I can't even begin to describe what is depicted so graphically in Mel Gibson's *The Passion of the Christ,* and if you haven't yet seen it, I strongly suggest that you view it and then start this book over.)

Having learned of the practice of crucifixion from barbarians, the Romans adopted it as a form of capital punishment for the worst of their criminals, but only for "nonpersons" and slaves. Virtually never was a Roman citizen crucified, except in the case of extreme treason. The term in the New Testament "now normally translated 'cross' denotes in Greek an instrument of torture and execution. . . . Two words are used for the instrument of execution on which Jesus died: *xylon* (wood, tree) and *stauros* (stake, cross)."[2]

Surprisingly, the cross didn't gain wide acceptance as a Christian symbol until nearly A.D. 200, but it was Roman Emperor Constantine who later branded it permanently in the heart of the church. History mixed with bits of legend tells us that before the critical battle of Milvian Bridge (early in the fourth century), Constantine had a vision of a lighted cross in the sky, accompanied with the words "By this sign you will conquer." After his great victory, the cross was emblazoned on the uniforms and battle flags of his legions.

The emblem of the cross, then, has evolved from a symbol of humiliation and shame, to a sign rich in significance, to an idolatrous object of worship and instrument of magic, and finally to broad, meaningless popularity as an accessory for rock bands and entertainers in the twenty-first century. Christianity is the largest religion in the world,[3] and the cross is doubtless the most widely used and recognized religious symbol in human history.

BLOOD

> There is a fountain filled with blood, Drawn from Emmanuel's veins. And sinners plunged beneath that flood lose all their guilty stains.
> —William Cowper

I once heard someone say that wherever you open the Bible it bleeds—it's a bloody book. Sacrifices. Countless animal sacrifices. It's an animal-rights activist's nightmare. How could they do that? *Why* did they kill all those animals? And then, horror of horrors, Jesus of Nazareth, the Son of God, went to the cross and shed his own blood for the forgiveness of our sins.

A human being, bleeding on a cross; the road to heaven is spattered with the blood of the Savior. Peter described Christians as "God's elect, strangers in the world . . . chosen according to the foreknowledge of God the Father, through the sanctifying work of the Spirit, for obedience to Jesus Christ and sprinkling by his blood."[4]

Is that wonderful?

Or is it disgusting?

It very much depends on your reality. Many people think the Bible's obsession with blood is outdated and overrated. Think about it. Really think about it: Every time we do Communion, the Lord's Supper, we remind ourselves that Jesus said, "This cup is the new testament *in my blood,* which is shed for [your sins]."[5] We do this so routinely that we hardly stop to think about the dreadful, bloody death of the Savior.

Have you ever seen someone bleeding? Bleeding profusely? Bleeding to death? Most people can handle seeing a basketball player bumped to the floor. Or a hockey player knocked unconscious. But if there's blood, a lot of blood, almost everyone watching goes silent. Or gets sick. Like watching the young medic in *Private Ryan* bleeding to death. Turning gray. Crying for his mother.

I was in Turkey with friends. We were speeding along a narrow road from the ancient city of Ephesus on our way to the ruins of Miletus, the very place where the apostle Paul said his earthly good-byes to some of his closest friends.[6] Ahead, just off the side of the ribbon of uneven asphalt, was a van. Upside down.

Slowing to a crawl, we edged by the small crowd gathered around the wreck and, like every person who gets really curious about accidents and disasters, I strained to see what had happened. I'm so sorry I did. An elderly woman who'd been struck by the van was lying in the middle of the road. I can still see her lifeless right hand, palm-side up, sticking out from under a blanket of newspapers. And the blood. Spilled onto the cold, filthy pavement was a huge pool of that dear woman's crimson life.

Shaken, I cried for her and her family.

I prayed.

It's in my memory forever.

BLOOD.

I may have made you feel uncomfortable, but I'm trying to make the bloody sacrifices of the Bible feel more real, to resurrect them from the grave of dead religious facts. When you see how many animal sacrifices the Israelites had to make and how bloody terminal they were, you'll have a much deeper appreciation for the priceless sacrifice of Jesus, the Lamb of God who takes away the sins of the world.[7]

PENANCE OR PUNISHMENT

So why did they kill all those animals? Why was that necessary? Why was this something *God* wanted? And if so, what kind of God would want that? Well, it has to do with the bottomless depravity of my soul. Not that I'm a terrible person, but I know I'm not what I should be, and I often have a deep sense of separation from God, even on my best days. It's why every human being feels a need for penance.

(No, I'm not thinking here in terms of the Catholic Sacrament of Penance. I will be using the term throughout this chapter in the more general sense of our felt need to make restitution for our failures.)

Our "sacrifices" for self-recognized sins range from roses to suicide. Recently I saw a sign on a flower shop marquis: "Done anything you feel guilty about lately?" If something pops into my mind, I can just make a hard right into the store lot, spend a hundred dollars on a bouquet, and kiss my guilt and shame good-bye! Well . . . until the next time I do something stupid.

Moving up the penance scale, people pray, go to church, give money to charitable organizations. We have people on our campus during the week doing court-mandated community service. Of course, you *should* do all these things for the *right* reasons, like giving someone flowers just because you love them! But many of the good things we do, including spiritual things, can be motivated by varying levels of guilt. On the extreme other end of the penance scale, people kill themselves. *Sacrifice* themselves. Like the young naval officer in the movie *Master and Commander* who, convinced he was bad karma for the crew, threw himself over the side of the ship. Tragically, these misguided souls act on a belief that self-inflicted death is the only way to self-atone for their wrongs.

Sooner or later, all of us feel shame because we haven't lived up to someone else's expectations. Usually we don't even live up to our own, so what about God? What does he expect of us, and how are we ever going to live up to that? What will happen to us when we don't? In our minds, there are essentially two options: penance or punishment. I either make up for what I've done, or I'm going to get nailed. What goes around comes around, unless I interrupt the cycle of sin and death by doing something good, something noble and praiseworthy.

Or maybe I just need to tell myself I'm not really a bad person. Maybe people do bad things mostly because they *think* they're bad, so if we can all just imagine that we're essentially good, all our badness will fade into the dark past of primitive religious ideas. Imagine that, Imagine no religion.

The problem, though, is that *other* people still drive like idiots. Shouldn't *they* get tickets and steep fines for their defiant foolishness? What if someone drives drunk . . . or drives drunk and kills someone?

Or just kills someone? Or rapes and kills someone? (This happened to a beautiful young woman in our church.)

Shouldn't there be justice in our world? While we're imagining a better life and visualizing world peace, should people who do bad (sinful?) things pay a penalty? Some people do things so heinous they couldn't make restitution if they had ten lifetimes. Sooner or later, then, every one of us will think, or we'll blurt it out in a moment of hostile indignation, "Those kinds of people should go to hell."

What in the world does that mean? *Where does that come from?* I'll tell you where. It's from the deep sense of justice written by God into the heart of every human being. Indeed, justice start with God himself:

> He has showed you, O man, what is good.
> And what does the LORD require of you?
> To act justly and to love mercy
> and to walk humbly with your God.
>
> MICAH 6:8

God's expectations for us are clear. And simple. And absolute. And out of reach.

You think not?

HELL ON THE FREEWAY

Speaking to an audience of "pretty good people," Jesus taught, "You have heard that it was said to the people long ago, 'Do not murder,'[8] and anyone who murders will be subject to judgment.'" Imagine their thinking, *Yeah, yeah. We've obeyed that commandment. Haven't killed anyone. This doesn't include us.*

Until Jesus adds, "But I tell you that anyone who is angry with his brother will be subject to judgment. Again, anyone who says to his brother, 'Raca,' [calls his brother a bad name] is answerable to the Sanhedrin [the Jewish court]. But anyone who says, 'You fool!' will be in danger of the fire of hell."[9] *What?!*

You mean I can be in danger of hell for calling someone else on the freeway a jerk? Yes. Jesus is teaching us that if you have a fit of rage and call someone a fool, *from God's point of view,* you've broken the sixth Commandment.[10] And in case this isn't clear, Jesus adds the better-known teaching: "You have heard that it was said, 'Do not commit adultery' [the seventh commandment[11]]. But I tell you that anyone who looks at woman lustfully [which pretty much includes every heterosexual male ever] has already committed adultery with her in his heart.

Or "If your right eye causes you to sin, gouge it out and throw it away. It is better for you to lose one part of your body than for your whole body to be thrown into hell."[12] In other words, mental adultery is so offensive to God that we're better off blind, because you lessen your chances of going to hell.

Well, it seems like we're back to the problem of really rigid religion. Actually not. Jesus is not, for heaven's sake, putting people down, or trying to make us feel guilty. Instead, he's simply doing his job identifying the problem. Like a good doctor, he's telling us that, from God's perspective, our condition is terminal and helpless. That somehow we should make up for our sin. Sacrifice animals. Do penance. But sadly, our effort is never enough, which is why Christ had to die, the ultimate and perfect bloody sacrifice for our sins once and forever.

WE NEED TO FACE REALITY EVEN IF IT BITES

Talking about our sin like this can be downright depressing. I was depressed just before the holidays when my doctor told me, "We're going to have to do a biopsy on that." Long silence. *I think I can't breathe.* "A biopsy?" I whisper. "You have to be kidding."

"No," he said. "I have to rule out cancer, even though it doesn't look like cancer."

For about a month, the C-word gave me cause to think deeply about a thing or two. I'm a pastor. I preach about these things, you know. Life and death. Time and eternity. But suddenly my daily reality seemed less real. It was a little like the moment in *The Matrix* right after Neo swallows the pill. It was as if my world was a delicate watercolor on a huge window, and somebody had a fire hose on it. All the colors of my future were streaking down the glass into a slimy puddle on the floor.

There I was, teetering in my soul between two realities, and on the other side of that glass was eternity. Paul said, "Now we see through a glass, darkly; but then face to face."[13] *The Message* reads,

> We don't yet see things clearly. We're squinting in a fog, peering through a mist. But it won't be long before the weather clears and the sun shines bright! We'll see it all then, see it all as clearly as God sees us, knowing him directly just as he knows us!

KILLIN' ME

Only weeks before I saw my doctor, my mother's physician told her she had a brain tumor the size of a lime. Fortunately, he also told her it wasn't malignant, but on Christmas Eve she was telling our kids that maybe she wouldn't be with us next year. What kind of a doctor would tell a great-grandmother she had a brain tumor? And during the holidays? Why, I simply can't believe in doctors like that! Doctors like that make me feel terrible about myself.

Catching my analogy? So often we hear similar comments about God: "I don't believe in a God like that." Like what? Like a doctor who would rather tell you the honest truth than see you die of cancer? Like a God who would rather tell you the honest truth than watch you go to hell? Even though hearing about cancer and hell can be so depressing?

Or what about those who say, "Maybe there really is a right and a wrong, and maybe there really is a heaven and a hell. But I don't like their tone of voice when religious people tell me about those things." Yeah, that's like saying, "If my doctor had only been more kind, more diplomatic when she told me about my cancer, I'd believe her. But she was too abrupt, so I'm just not going to believe I have cancer." Dumb.

The truth is the truth. *Alétheia is alétheia.* How ever you want to talk about it, reality is reality. If I have cancer, I *must* know. Without a correct diagnosis, treatment is meaningless. So when Jesus tells me I'm close to hell when I look at a woman the wrong way, he's telling me I have a deeply rooted problem, which the Bible simply calls *sin*.

Sin is like cancer. It's me killing me. My bad cells taking on my good cells. Without radical intervention, bad cells win. And I don't have a clue I'm dying until the doctor tells me. I guess I should be mad at the doctor. Must be his fault.

The Bible makes it real simple: "All have sinned and fall short of the glory of God."[14] *Sin* here is a Greek word that means, basically, "to miss the mark," not a religious word so much as a word about arrows missing the center of the target. Anything short, or right or left of the bull's-eye "misses the mark."[15] Sin is God's diagnosis of the human condition, but he's not telling us about our problem to make us feel like scum—*he's telling us so we'll get treatment.*

DIAGNOSIS: The Cancer of Sin

Treatment Options:

1. Believe your doctor and do nothing. Let the cancer (sin) run its course.

   - **Side effects:** Consequences, justice, judgment . . . hell, here and now, and maybe later.

2. Stomp out of the office and find another doctor. Find another God. Modify the God you have. Find a God who is "kinder, gentler," less forthright.

   - **Side effects:** You feel better now, but in the end cancer wins.

3. Treat yourself. Penance. Give up coffee and beer. Drink gallons of carrot juice every day. Go back to church.

   - **Side effects:** Dizziness from running in religious circles, as suggested by this Scripture: "Will the LORD be pleased with thousands of rams, with ten thousand rivers of oil? Shall I offer my firstborn for my transgression, the fruit of my body for the sin of my soul?"[16]

4. **Radical surgery.** Cut out the cancer. Start life over. Listen carefully to the doctor's words: "I've made a way to take the cancer out of you and put it in me. I know this sounds wacked, but I can die instead of you, in your place. I'll let your cancer kill me. In the end, I'll be okay. You'll see."

   - **Side effects:** You have to believe the doctor, which can be difficult if you've already make up your mind about what's wrong with you, if you're living in the matrix of self-delusion. And you'll have to say yes to the doctor. It will hurt. There will probably be a long rehab, which will make you think from time to time that maybe it would have been better to leave the cancer alone.

GOTTA LIKE MY CHANCES

Just last week the specialist who did the biopsy told me he'd developed a procedure with which he's had 100 percent success. *100 percent!* After he told me I also had other options, I asked, "So if you were me, you'd do the special procedure?" He surprised me by saying, "I'm not telling you what to do, I'm just giving you options."

He has 100 percent success doing one thing, partial success doing other things, and if I want, I have the right to choose partial success? Yeah, right! But a funny thing happened as I sat there in his office: I paused to consider the choices. I know he said his special treatment works *every* time, but then . . . well . . . I started doubting: *Maybe it doesn't.*

God's diagnosis of the human condition is accurate, and his treatment is successful 100 percent of the time. God never misdiagnoses or misprescribes. God doesn't just tell us how bad we are and leave us there. He offers us his unconditional love in the sacrifice of his Son.

This is how much God loved the world: He gave his Son, his one and only Son. And this is why: so that no one need be destroyed; by believing in him, anyone can have a whole and lasting life.

God didn't go to all the trouble of sending his Son merely

to point an accusing finger, telling the world how bad it was. He came to help, to put the world right again. Anyone who trusts in him is acquitted; anyone who refuses to trust him has long since been under the death sentence without knowing it.

JOHN 3:16–18 THE MESSAGE

I want to believe in *this* God!

God gave his one and only Son, and it was a bloody mess. Human life rebelled against God and fell into sin. Something had to be done. God could have started over, but for reasons raveled in mystery, he chose another path. In the Edenic haze of the primeval world, God contemplated his options. He looked at Adam and Eve, and then for a moment on Moriah when Abraham raised the knife to kill his only son. Past the countless bloody, screaming sacrifices of Hebrew religion. Beyond a star, over Bethlehem to the Place of the Skull, Golgatha, where he, God, would die in the Person of his Son, Jesus Christ.

> How could anyone look at the cross and see only the shame of what it did to Christ rather than the glory of what he did for us?
>
> —John Stott

Then and there, as Adam and Eve stood cowering before him, God foretold of a cataclysmic encounter between good and evil. To the serpent, the god of evil, he declared, "I will put enmity between you and the woman, and between your offspring and hers; he will crush your head, and you will strike his heel."[17] Looking back, we know now what God had in mind: a plan of salvation through a chosen people and finally in the Son of David, the Savior.

CROSS POINTS

So back to an earlier question: *Why did they kill all those animals?* The New Testament book of Hebrews, an overview of God's plan, explains the relationship between the Old Testament Scriptures and the New Testament Scriptures; between the first part of the plan (the Jewish old covenant) and the final part of the plan (the Christian new covenant); between the limitations of the ancient sacrificial system and the consummate sacrifice of God's Son. Below are a few of the main points of Hebrews 10. (I highly recommend that you read Hebrews 10 before reading on in this chapter.)

First, *all the Old Testament sacrifices are a shadow of Christ.* The Savior's future work is hidden in their rich spiritual meaning: "The law is only a shadow of the good things that are coming—not the realities themselves."[18]

Second, *the year-after-year-after-year sacrifices sent a message: you're forgiven for now but not forever.* A mountain of good works, a lifetime of penance will never take away guilt.

> [Old Testament ceremonial law] *can never,* by the same sacrifices repeated endlessly year after year, *make perfect*[19] those who draw near to worship. If it could, would they not have stopped being offered? For the worshipers would have been cleansed once for all, and would no longer have felt guilty for their sins. But those sacrifices are an annual reminder of sins, because it is impossible for the blood of bulls and goats to take away sins.
>
> HEBREWS 10:1–4, EMPHASIS MINE

> By one sacrifice he [Christ] has made perfect forever those who are being made holy.
> —Hebrews 10:14

Third, *from the first sacrifice, God knew there was only one cure for the cancer of sin: the death of his own Son:* "Therefore, when Christ came into the world, he said: 'Sacrifice and offering you did not desire . . . with burnt offerings and sin offerings you were not pleased.'"[20]

Fourth, *Christ died once and forever, because his sacrifice was perfect.*

We have been made holy through the sacrifice of the body of Jesus Christ *once for all.*

Day after day every priest stands and performs his religious duties; again and again he offers the same sacrifices, which can never take away sins. But when this priest [Jesus Christ] had offered for all time [forever] *one* sacrifice [and only one, because it was perfect] for sins, he *sat down* at the right hand of God.

HEBREWS 10:10–12, EMPHASIS MINE

He sat down because his work was finished . . . complete . . . perfect.

Fifth, *the sacrifice of Jesus makes it possible for us to become perfect forever.* Imagine a new reality, a world where everything is perfect, faultless, and whole. Only in that world is there no injustice, no failure, no shame, no need for penance or punishment, no judgment, and no hell. Ever. This has to be one of the most extraordinary statements in the Bible: "By one sacrifice he [Christ] has made perfect forever those who are being made holy."[21] Note the realities in contrast, like day and night, east and west, North Pole and Amazon Basin. Two worlds, two realities:

- Reality #1: Penance[22] *"can never,* by the same sacrifices repeated endlessly year after year, *make perfect* those who draw near to worship." This is why people eventually give up on formal religion.

- Reality #2: "By *one* sacrifice he [Jesus] has made *perfect forever* those who are being made holy." This sums up the purpose of Christ's death and the whole of the Christian life. This is why God never gives up on us.

"PERFECT"

Let's camp here for a while. First, we have to talk about "perfect." It's not what you think: perfect like a brand-new car without a scratch. Frankly, the English word is weak. But the Greek term, a derivative of *telos,* is bursting with meaning and significance, especially in the way it's used of Jesus. *Telos* has the sense of complete, mature, whole. *Telos* is the end, the conclusion, the last part, the goal. We might say *telos* is consummation, the final destination and ultimate reality. The verb form, *teleioô,* means "to bring to an end, to complete, to accomplish, to fulfill."[23]

How significant is this word? It's the very last thing Jesus said on the cross before he died: *tetelestai,* "It is finished."[24] Ponder this! At the very end of Christ's life, after he'd done *everything* he came to accomplish, as he was taking his last breath, he declared, "It is finished, it is done." Or, *"Everything has now been made perfect."*

On the third day God raised him from the dead. Forty days later he ascended into heaven and *"sat down* at the right hand of God."[25] You understand, of course, that when people sit down at the end of the day (desk jobs weren't common at the time of Christ), their work is done, there's nothing more to do. Following the logic? When we believe *into* Christ, he becomes our new reality. His perfect sacrifice is enough to cover all our sins. There's nothing more he needs to do and nothing more we need to do.

"FOREVER"

But there's more. Not only has Christ made me perfect, he's made me perfect *forever,* which in itself is a unique and comprehensive Greek expression. It means "for all time, continually, perpetually and uninterrupted." To make this even more potent, in both places where we are considering this word,[26] the terms are in the perfect tense,[27] which deepens and intensifies their meaning. In other words, "it has been and forever will remain finished."[28] Jesus, then, is absolutely the ultimate sacrifice. Jesus has perfectly perfected us forever!

Sixth, *permanent change on the inside changes us on the outside.* Take one more look at this affirmation, particularly the final phrase: "By one sacrifice he has made perfect forever *those who are being made holy."* This refers to the outcome of being made perfect in Christ. As a result of inwardly being made perfect, we now have the freedom and power to change on the outside, to be "made holy."

God sees holiness in us because he sees Christ in us, but what's evident to God is not always evident to us and to our friends. We may have believed into Christ, but the way we act at times, well, you wouldn't know it. The path to spiritual maturity, becoming more like Christ, is what the Bible calls sanctification.

As we've seen, being born again, entering into the perfect reality of Christ (*justification*), happens once and forever, but *sanctification,* being made holy, is a day-by-day process. Paul surely had this mind when he wrote, "Continue to work out your salvation with fear and trembling, for it is God who works in you to will and to act according to his good purpose."[29] Notice that he doesn't tell us to work *for* our salvation, or to work *on* it, but to work it *out,* to move the perfection of Christ in us from what God sees to what others see.

TATTOOS ON MY MIND

Seventh, *"perfect forever"* is only possible if the One who did all the right things at all the right times for all the right reasons is somehow placed inside my very own heart.[30] Instead of God having to break the hard stone tablets of the Ten Commandments over my head, instead of God's holy finger pointing at my unholy face, his holy hand reaches inside my head and tattoos the Ten Commandments on my brain:

> The Holy Spirit also testifies to us about this. First, he says: This is the covenant I will make with them after that time, says the Lord.
> *I will put my laws in their hearts,* and I will write them on their minds. . . . Their sins and lawless acts *I will remember no more.*
> And where these have been forgiven, there is *no longer any sacrifice* for sin.
>
> HEBREWS 10:16–18, EMPHASIS MINE

In other words, Christ's perfect sacrifice initiated the new covenant, a New Reality, which the prophet Jeremiah foretold centuries earlier. This new covenant would be characterized by three things:

- Spiritual transformation will happen from the inside out, instead of expecting organized religion to change people outside in.[31]

- Sins will be forgiven forever,[32] which means that . . .

- Sacrifice will no longer be necessary.[33]

At this point, may I remind you of something I wrote in the second chapter: Partaking of Jesus is like swallowing the red pill in *The Matrix.* Recall that in the gospel of John, Jesus says, "Whoever eats my flesh and drinks my blood has eternal life, and I will raise him up at the last day. For my flesh is real food and my blood is real drink."[34]

Whether or not Jesus is speaking directly about Holy Communion here has been a matter of debate. We do know, however, that when Jesus offered his disciples the bread and the cup at the Last Supper, he said,

> "Take and eat; *this is my body.*" Then he took the cup, gave thanks and offered it to them, saying, "Drink from it, all of you. *This is my blood of the covenant,* which is poured out for many *for the forgiveness of sins.*"
>
> MATTHEW 26:26–28, EMPHASIS MINE

In the gospel of Luke, the words are slightly different: "'This cup is the *new covenant* in my blood.'"[35] Notice these key words and phrases:

- "this is my blood of the covenant"
- "for the forgiveness of sins"
- "the new covenant in my blood"

Amazing! None of his words in the Upper Room was accidental. Jesus was making it unmistakably clear that he and he alone could initiate the new covenant, which is precisely what Hebrews 10 teaches us.

LET'S NOT PASS OVER THIS

In the Upper Room, the night before his crucifixion, Jesus was linking himself with the hidden meaning of the Passover and God's covenant with Israel. According to Exodus, after a number of hideous plagues sent from God (including billions of flies, gnats, and frogs) to put pressure on the Egyptians, Pharaoh would still not let the Hebrew slaves leave. "Okay," God said to Moses, "this is it. After tonight Pharaoh will finally make up his mind. Before the sun rises in the morning, the angel of death will fly through the land, taking the lives of every firstborn child and beast.

"My protection and deliverance for you is the blood of the lamb. Tonight every Hebrew home must kill a lamb, as good a lamb as they can find, and with the blood drained from that lamb's body, I want your people to mark their dwellings, three bloody spots on the three sides of the doorframe. When the angel of judgment sees the blood on your house, he will *pass over,* and your children will be spared."[36]

That night as the angel of death did his terrible work, shrieks of agony and despair could be heard all through the land of Egypt. In the morning, Pharaoh let God's people go, and every spring ever since—for about thirty-five hundred years—Jews have observed the Passover. Not accidentally, on the night before Jesus was crucified in bloody sacrifice to set us free from slavery to sin, he sat down with his disciples and celebrated the Passover. It was his Last Supper, not only because he did not eat again until after his death and resurrection, but also because by establishing the *new* covenant sealed in *his* blood, he was nullifying the animal sacrifices of the old covenant.

That very night thousands of Jews, who had come to Jerusalem from all over the world for this holy festival, were slaughtering lambs in bloody sacrifice. And that night, the night of the Passover, Jesus presented his disciples with the cup of "the new covenant in my blood." Little did the vast crowds in Jerusalem know that what was happening in a candlelit room would end the need for animal sacrifice forever. O holy night, the stars were brightly shining. It was the night before our dear Savior's death.

Jesus' Jewish disciples also certainly must have understood that his words, "This is my blood of the covenant for the forgiveness of sins," echoed the proclamation of Moses, the father of the old covenant established at Mount Sinai. Right after coming down from the mountain,

> Moses then wrote down everything the LORD had said. He got up early the next morning and built an altar at the foot of the mountain and set up twelve stone pillars representing the twelve tribes of Israel. Then he sent young Israelite men, and they offered burnt offerings and sacrificed young bulls as fellowship offerings to the LORD.
>
> Moses took half of the blood and put it in bowls, and the other half he sprinkled on the altar. Then he took the Book of the [old] covenant and read it to the people. . . . Moses then took the blood, sprinkled it on the people and said,

"This is the blood of the covenant that the LORD has made with you."

EXODUS 24:4–8

This is almost word for word what Jesus said to his disciples at the Last Supper! When Jesus introduced his disciples to the *new* reality in *his* blood, he made that old reality go away forever.

Eighth, and finally, *when you're perfect—that is, when you know your sins are forgiven—every step of the journey of your life will be free of shame and full of confident hope for your future.* When you're perfect, you don't ever have to worry about getting into trouble with your Father:

> Therefore, brothers, since we have confidence to enter the Most Holy Place by the blood of Jesus, by a new and living way opened for us through the curtain, that is, his body, and since we have a great priest over the house of God, let us draw near to God with a sincere heart in full assurance of faith, having our hearts sprinkled to cleanse us from a guilty conscience and having our bodies washed with pure water. Let us hold unswervingly to the hope we profess, for he who promised is faithful.
>
> HEBREWS 10:19–23

No doubt there is a sense of journey in this final text in our encounter with Hebrews 10, a journey into a most holy place of personal freedom, a journey into a new reality of unconditional *perfect* love, acceptance, and forgiveness.

And the journey continues. . . .

FOR REFLECTION AND DISCUSSION

Read Hebrews 10:1–18. In what areas of your life do you wrestle with feelings of inadequacy? What are some of the things you do for "penance"?

What are some things you can do to redirect your focus away from your own limitations to the perfect finished work of Christ on the cross? In what ways do you think this will bring about greater freedom in your life?

PART TWO

Cross Purposes

TURNOUTS

You know it's a huge church when the entrance into the parking lot has a place to pull over and take photos. And, for a quarter, a view through a telescope. "Wow!" (not "Praise the Lord!") was my initial response the first time I drove onto the Willow Creek Community Church property northwest of Chicago. I'm the senior pastor of a large church, and friends have said "Wow!" when I've showed them our worship center, but my "Wow!" was based on a Greek word that means "I couldn't have imagined a church like this if I tried."

Actually, there's no such Greek term, but that's how I felt. Oh, and Willow Creek doesn't have a telescope, but they do have a turnout for panoramic snapshots of their massive corporate-center-like facility just beyond their not-so-small lake. If you're a pastor, it's one place to pause for a reality check.

Here in Phoenix, at the end of a busy city street, is a secluded prayer garden on the property of Canaan in the Desert, a faith community of the Evangelical Sisterhood of Mary.[1] I suppose you could call it a Protestant convent. Willow Creek is one expression of the kingdom of God, this place is a very different one. I've been to Canaan several times to write. And to pray.

Along the paths of this desert retreat are sculptures and reliefs representing moments in our Savior's passion. Benches invite worshipers to pause and contemplate what each element of Christ's suffering means. Today I found a simple, lovely Web site that, using Scripture and striking illustrations, presents the twelve primary events, or "stations," of the Passion.[2]

Some people might feel uncomfortable expressing their spirituality in this way, maybe thinking that it seems "Catholic," or that we shouldn't spend so much time praying about the Crucifixion (after all, Jesus is risen!), or that this would tend to focus on negative things, like suffering and death. These reactions are unfortunate, because Christ-followers, especially we who live in sheltered North America, know so little about what it means to bear our cross, to lay down our lives and walk in the Master's footsteps.

As we reflect on Christ—his work on the Cross and his Word—our lives are transformed. Unlike what we expect from microwaves and DSL—*speed*—walking with God slows down the pace of our life. To follow Christ is to crucify our self-destructive passions, one of which is our relentless restlessness.

Did you know that the singular purpose of the marketing industry is to inject a sense of need and discontent? In countless creative ways, advertisers tell us that we're missing something if we don't buy their product or service. The more advertising intrudes into our lives, the more restless and unsatisfied we feel. And we don't even know why. A weapon of mass discontent, advertising is what keeps our consumer-driven world turning.

VIEWPOINTS AHEAD

Here's a way out of matrix madness: You can step into the reality of Christ by taking time to contemplate prayerfully what I've come to believe are the seven most significant outcomes of his work on the cross. If you're wondering, "Only seven?" yes, I agree that so much more could be said about what Jesus did for us in his death. Right about the time Mel Gibson released *The Passion of the Christ*, for example, John Piper wrote a book in which he gives *fifty* specific reasons why Jesus died.[3] What I offer here is a simple practical theology of the Cross. Please don't think of these next few chapters as a teaching outline. My prayer for you, my reader, is for this book to be a source of life and a map for your journey. While I'm hoping to answer some questions, my greater goal is to help you engage in a heartfelt dialogue with Jesus himself.

As you read on, consider these chapters as places to stop and take in the view. Right now I'm writing at an isolated retreat center just a few miles from the world-famous red rocks of Sedona, Arizona. People around here say that God created the Grand Canyon but lives in Sedona. Both places are magnificent, and every turn in the road is a viewpoint.

Slow down! Turn out of your speeding world and coast into God's reality. Stop! Take it in! Let God show you more about himself and his creation. Take time to encounter God and believe into the reality of Christ.

Philip Mitchell, assistant professor of English at Dallas Baptist University, writes,

> When I reflect on Christ's words on the cross, I am struck how he acted through his words: he requested; he commanded; he promised; he questioned, and he fulfilled. With each sentence, he showed us both his human and divine natures. He provided for his mother, suffered, cared for a repentant criminal, and yet felt the sacrifice that tore at the heart of the Godhead. He also provided for all humanity.
>
> I am also struck by my own unworthiness to speak to these sayings. How can I fathom the depths of such a mystery as God dying for me? And this is why I need both commentary and meditation, for words so rich and profound need a lifetime to understand and live with. No one person alone can fully plumb them.[4]

You can speed-read this section and get on with urgent and pressing things (not recommended), or you can drive for the drive's sake. You may want to journal your way through these seven viewpoints (in the next seven chapters). I strongly urge you, if at all possible, to use these turnouts as points of meditation, prayer, and Bible study alone—or with a few friends—during Lent, the seven weeks leading up to Easter.

CHAPTER FIVE

The Problem With Hell

Viewpoint #1:
The Cross is the exit door from the penalty of sin.

Be assured that when God curses, it is a curse of the most weighty kind.

—Charles Spurgeon

Life without God is hell.

What hell looks like, feels like, we can only guess. Jesus described it in terms of Jerusalem's worst garbage dump, Gehenna, a ravine south of the city where people threw everything from Twinkie wrappers to animal carcasses. It smelled nasty, and in order to manage the tons of garbage brought there weekly, they kept it burning day and night.

I've had meat scraps cooking in my City of Mesa garbage barrel on 112 degree summer days here in Arizona. *Whew! Really* bad! I feel like gagging just thinking about it. Imagine climbing inside my trash bin on its worst day. Step into my oozing meat, pull down the lid, and sit there in sweltering darkness for a few hours. Imagine spending years in there.

Gehenna. It was the last place on earth you would want to be, except to add your own stinking trash to the top of the smoldering pile.[1] No one would ever stay there, live there. Yet this is the way Jesus described the judgment *of* God and separation *from* God.

I know the idea of an angry God is not real popular, but it's not that God is mad in a road-rage sort of way. God's rage is more outrage because of what individuals do to themselves and to one another. I find it hard to understand why people find it hard to believe in a God of justice, when all of us are enraged by inhumane human behavior.

EVIL IS SO WRONG

C. S. Lewis points out in his classic book *Mere Christianity* that we may argue hotly about what exactly is right and what exactly is wrong, but no one in his right mind suggests that there is no such thing as right and wrong. Some may not use words like *right, wrong,* and *sin,* but we have our substitutes: *unjust, inappropriate, unacceptable, objectionable, illegal.*

Tell me, what do these words mean if they don't represent a departure from some norm or standard? What word do you use to describe what happened on September 11, 2001? Was it merely "inappropriate" for terrorists to slam planes into defenseless public buildings and kill thousands of innocent people?

Or was President Bush correct in calling the shocking events "evil"?

Some people didn't like hearing the E-word. Is it wrong to call something evil? Is that too judgmental? Or is it judgmental to tell someone they're being judgmental?

Some people believe abortion is perfectly acceptable. But what about a teenage migrant worker who doesn't want her baby and doesn't know how to work the system? Who can't even speak English? What do we do with her when she throws her newborn child into a portable toilet at a lakeside park? That's exactly what happened a few years ago here in Arizona. Millions in Phoenix shared stunned outrage, but if she'd been able to get an abortion a few weeks earlier, community indignance wouldn't have been heard over the sound of a purring cat.

You see, we human beings have a deep sense of conscience, of guilt, of shame, of insult, of outrage. When something horrific happens, like 9/11 or kids killing other kids in a high school in Littleton, Colorado, we all cry out for justice . . . and justice is in perfect harmony with the word and heart of God.

If we Americans can be angry over the right things, and if we expect justice for terrorists and wanton criminals, why shouldn't God be outraged about sin in his universe? He is: "The wrath of God is being revealed from heaven against all the godlessness and wickedness of men who suppress the truth by their wickedness."[2]

SINS TO DIE FOR

All this sin-and-hell business started ages ago when God said to Adam, "You must not eat from the tree of the knowledge of good and evil, for when you eat of it you will surely die."[3] From the very beginning God made it clear that there would be consequences for doing wrong things, specifically for disobeying his word.

I've often thought about how the entire cosmos is saturated with a sense of right and wrong, bound by both natural and spiritual laws of cause-and-effect. Jump off a tall building, and you will probably die. Oh, you might not, but then the chances of survival aren't very good. Sleep around, and it will probably affect you some way physically or emotionally. Oh, it might not, but chances are pretty good it will.

The wages of sin is death in all its forms: emotional, physical, intellectual, relational, spiritual. Just as a misunderstanding can lead to the death of a friendship, or adultery can result in the death of a marriage, so my sin nature separates me from God. Every sin I commit has the potential to create its own private hell:

> Do not be deceived: God cannot be mocked. A man reaps
> what he sows. The one who sows to please his sinful nature,
> from that nature will reap destruction; the one who sows to
> please the Spirit, from the Spirit will reap eternal life.
>
> GALATIANS 6:7–8

Paul wrote to the young church in Rome,

What benefit did you reap at that time from the things you are now ashamed of? *Those things result in death!* But now that you have been set free from sin and have become slaves to God, the benefit you reap leads to holiness, and the result is eternal life. For the wages of sin is death.

In bold contrast he adds: *"The gift of God is eternal life in Christ Jesus our Lord."*[4]

According to the Bible, the consummate penalty for sin is eternal separation from God: hell. I asked Chris Wolfard, my friend and colleague of many years, why he believed in hell, and his answer surprised me: "If there is no hell," he replied, "why was Jesus crucified?"

Perhaps the most memorable of Christ's words on the cross were, "'Eloi, Eloi, lama sabachthani?'—which means, 'My God, my God, why have you forsaken me?'"[5] Scholars have pondered possible reasons why Jesus said this, but probably the most commonly held view (which has also been mine for years) is that Jesus literally went to hell in that moment. If we define hell simply as the absence of God, that's certainly what Christ was experiencing.

The Apostles' Creed states that Jesus was "crucified, dead, and buried. He descended into hell." This latter statement is based on a mysterious New Testament text that refers to Jesus preaching to imprisoned spirits in the underworld.[6] This was not, however, the moment of Christ's God-forsakenness, which some call "the cry of dereliction." John Calvin wrote,

> Our sin must be extremely horrible. Nothing reveals the gravity of sin like the cross.
> —John Stott

If Christ had died only a bodily death, it would have been ineffectual. . . . Unless his soul shared in the punishment, he would have been the Redeemer of bodies alone. . . . He paid a greater and more excellent price in suffering in his soul the terrible torments of a condemned and forsaken man.[7]

Mind-boggling as this may seem, Jesus took upon himself our sin—he literally *became* sin—and as a consequence suffered the wrath and judgment of God on our behalf. "God made him who had no sin to be sin for us, so that in him we might become the righteousness of God."[8]

Jesus was forsaken and lost so we can be found.
Jesus died so we can live.
Jesus became sin so we can become righteous.
Jesus went unforgiven so we can be forgiven.
Jesus went to hell so we can go to heaven.

CROSS WORDS

Substitution. It was as a substitute that Jesus made this sacrifice; he took the place of the condemned. He acted on our behalf, as our representative in regard to sin, precisely because we are powerless to do it ourselves. To act on our behalf is to act as our substitute, to act in our place.
—2 Corinthians 5:14

Punishment. Jesus endured a punishment by becoming our substitute. Being handed over by his own people to the pagan occupying power was perceived as a mark of judgment: He fell under God's curse. It is important to see here the actual in-the-body acceptance of judgment by an absolutely righteous man for the sake of those who deserved to be forsaken.
—Isaiah 53

Propitiation. This word means an action that turns aside anger or wrath from a sinner. The Scriptures speak of God's wrath, his holy anger against sin and those who sin against him. His anger is just and thoroughly righteous; we deserved it. If there were no anger of God in this universe, we would be living in an unjust and hopeless world.
—1 John 2:2[9]

PRIESTS ON TRIAL

For God's sake, I need to be forgiven. In other words, forgiveness is more about God than it is about me. As much as I need to be released from the penalty of my sins and experience God's mercy and love, forgiveness is something he has to do for himself. Not that God has an emotional problem. It's not like he's learning anger-management skills. *God is a perfect judge, the source of perfect justice.* He is bound by the law of his own nature to uphold the law. More than something I need to feel in my heart, forgiveness is a legal necessity.

Sometimes we use the word *guilt* as a synonym for shame, as in, "I feel so guilty." Guilt actually has a more technical meaning, like when a jury solemnly announces its verdict. The former Catholic bishop of Phoenix, Thomas O'Brien, was convicted of leaving the scene of a fatal accident. Having struck an intoxicated pedestrian in the dark of night, but thinking someone had thrown a brick at his car, the church leader sped home. Details and images of his trial were splashed daily across the front page of the newspaper, and on the final day a photographer caught the bishop's sad, sagging face at the precise moment the hushed jury read its verdict: "Guilty."

I hurt deeply for Thomas, guilty or not. I had come to know him personally over the years, and he has sent me personal notes of appreciation for our acquaintance. There was nothing I could do except pray. "Guilty" in a court of law means consequences.

> Therefore, if anyone is in Christ, he is a new creation; the old has gone, the new has come! . . . God made him who had no sin to be sin for us, so that in him we might become the righteousness of God.
> —2 Corinthians 5:17, 21

Guilt, then, isn't just what I feel—it has a judicial[10] element. The Old Testament prophet Zechariah had a vision of another holy man in court:

> Joshua the high priest standing before the angel of the LORD, and Satan [the prosecuting attorney] standing at his right side to accuse him. The LORD said to Satan, "The LORD rebuke you, Satan! The LORD, who has chosen Jerusalem, rebuke you! Is not this man a burning stick snatched from the fire?"
>
> —3:1–2

Joshua was wearing filthy clothes. No trial by jury this time. Joshua was standing in the very presence of God, and Satan was pointing his long, fire-blackened finger in his face. Joshua didn't have a chance in hell. Being a pretty good person wasn't enough, and being the high priest of Israel wasn't enough. Joshua was guilty, period.

But the angel of the Lord, thought by many Bible teachers to be an Old Testament glimpse of the second person of the Trinity, Jesus

Christ, "said to those who were standing before him, 'Take off his filthy clothes.' Then he said to Joshua, "'See, *I have taken away your sin.'"[11] Joshua needed more than a good defense—he needed an intervention. He didn't need someone to go to bat for him—he needed someone to die for him.

> The forgiveness of sins does not pertain to particulars, as if on the whole one were good. . . . No . . . it pertains to the totality. It pertains to one's whole self, which is sinful and corrupts everything as soon as it comes in the slightest contact with it.
> —Søren Kierkegaard

Centuries earlier King David, author of many of the psalms, declared, "As far as the east is from the west, so far has he [God] removed our transgressions from us."[12] Centuries later when John the Baptist, preaching in the desert, saw Jesus in the crowd, he burst out, "Look, the Lamb of God, who takes away the sins of the world!"[13] Praise be to God! Not only does Jesus forgive our sins, he also removes them!

BOATS, ARROWS, AND SIN

This, in fact, is the primary sense of the Greek terms meaning "forgive" and "forgiveness" (*aphiémi*) throughout the New Testament. More precisely, *aphiémi* means "to release, to let go." A ship untied from its moorings is "forgiven"; an arrow released from the bow is "forgiven."[14] When Jesus forgives us, our sins are taken away, and we are released from their penalty, power, guilt, and shame.

But there's more. Not only does the Angel of the Lord take away our filthy garments, he also exchanges them for his perfectly clean robes of righteousness, without spot or wrinkle: "I will put rich garments on you," he says to Joshua the High Priest.[15] Paul provides new covenant perspective:

> Christ loved the church and gave himself up for her to make her holy, cleansing her by the washing with water through the word, and to present her to himself as a radiant church, without stain or wrinkle or any other blemish, but holy and blameless.

EPHESIANS 5:25–27

Our sin condemns us, damns us. As an alternative to sending all of sinful humanity to a hell that was created for the devil and his angels,[16] God sent his own Son to die, to be punished for the sins of the world. On the cross, Christ was condemned, damned on our behalf. Jesus' death, then, *releases* (*aphiémi*) us from the penalty of sin—we are acquitted, dismissed from the courtroom, as God forgives us. The Bible calls this "legal"[17] act "justification."[18] Some have pointed out that in order to remember the meaning of this theological term, note that to be "justified" is for God to see us made perfect in Christ, *just-as-if-I'd* never sinned.

> To face the deep and furious wrath of an infinite God even for an instant would cause the most profound fear. But Jesus' suffering was not over in a minute—or two— or ten. When would it end? Could there be yet more weight of sin? Yet more wrath of God? Hour after hour it went on—the dark weight of sin and the deep wrath of God poured over Jesus in wave after wave.
> —Wayne Grudem

Sin separates us from God. God's forgiveness separates us from sin. Imagine: God accepts you so unconditionally that when he sees you it's as if you never rebelled against him. Only a perfect God can forgive you perfectly.

INSTRUCTIONS FOR USING THE BIBLE READINGS AT THE END OF THIS AND THE FOLLOWING CHAPTERS

Lent begins on Ash Wednesday, six weeks before Easter. Ash Wednesday through Easter spans forty-six days. I've broken with tradition by providing *forty-nine* Bible readings, seven at the end of each chapter, for the seven weeks inclusive of Lent and Easter. In each of the seven Scripture lists, for the Friday reading, I've included one of the Seven Sayings of Christ on the Cross. I suggest that you look up these sayings, as well as the other passages I've given you, and contemplate them in their full contexts.

Note the cross symbols in the left margins at the end of this and the next six chapters. The number represents the week, and the letter represents the day of the week. For example, "1M" represents the

Monday prior to Ash Wednesday, the first week of Lent; "1Tu" is the first Tuesday, "2W" is the second Wednesday, and so on.

Viewpoint #1
The Cross is the exit door from the penalty of sin.

SCRIPTURE

†1M "Surely he took up our infirmities and carried our sorrows, yet we considered him stricken by God, smitten by him, and afflicted.

"But he was pierced for our transgressions, he was crushed for our iniquities; the punishment that brought us peace was upon him, and by his wounds we are healed.

"We all, like sheep, have gone astray, each of us has turned to his own way; and the LORD has laid on him the iniquity of us all."[19]

†1Tu "An angel of the Lord appeared to him in a dream and said, 'Joseph son of David, do not be afraid to take Mary home as your wife, because what is conceived in her is from the Holy Spirit. She will give birth to a son, and you are to give him the name Jesus, because he will save his people from their sins.'"[20]

†1W (Ash Wednesday) "John saw Jesus coming toward him and said, 'Look, the Lamb of God, who takes away the sin of the world!'"[21]

†1Th "All have sinned and fall short of the glory of God, and are justified freely by his grace through the redemption that came by Christ Jesus. God presented him as a sacrifice of atonement, through faith in his blood."[22]

†1F "'Eloi, Eloi, lama sabachthani?'—which means, 'My God, my God, why have you forsaken me?'"[23]

†1Sa "God so loved the world that he gave his one and only Son,

that whoever believes in him shall not perish but have eternal life."[24]

† 1 Su "As high as the heavens are above the earth, so great is his love for those who fear him; as far as the east is from the west, so far has he removed our transgressions from us."[25]

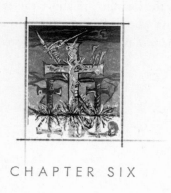

CHAPTER SIX

Shame on You

Viewpoint #2:
The Cross is the exit door from sin's pain: guilt and shame.

The anguished conscience alone understands Christ.
   —Søren Kierkegaard

I am ashamed of myself and renounce myself, and choose you, for
I can please neither you nor myself except in you.
   —Augustine, *Confessions*

"Guilty!"

Every head turned to stare at the defendant, who sat stone-faced
as the crack of the gavel echoed in the courtroom. The evidence
against him was incontestable, but the man felt nothing. Sentenced to
death, he felt no shame. Soft sobbing stabbed the silence. Someone in
the gallery knew him, loved him.

We all have a sin problem, and "we will all stand before God's judgment seat."[1] Legally speaking, we are all guilty, and our sin, our guilt, separates us from God. Jesus said of the Holy Spirit, "When he comes, he will convict the world of guilt in regard to sin and righteousness and judgment."[2]

One day God's gavel will thunder in the heavens, and every one of us will have to give an account. The incredibly good news, though, is that God loves the world so much that he gave us a way out of our deserved punishment: He sent his perfect, sinless Son as a substitute criminal.

> God was reconciling the world to himself in Christ, not
> counting men's sins against them. . . . God made him who
> had no sin to be sin for us, so that in him we might become
> the righteousness of God.
>
> 2 CORINTHIANS 5:19, 21

In heaven's courtroom, Jesus bore the penalty for our transgressions. Imagine your defense attorney being guilty for you, getting the death penalty because of something you did.

The word *guilt* is commonly used to describe how we feel about ourselves when we've done something wrong. Our sin-tainted souls *feel* guilty. While Christ's death legally releases me from sin's penalty— separation from God—the Cross of Christ also offers me freedom from my *experience* of guilt and shame. Reversing the curse, the Cross is our return ticket to Eden, where "the man and his wife were both naked, *and they felt no shame.*"[3]

People can feel shame even when they have no guilt. I've felt guilty about wrong things I've done (good), but I've also felt ashamed for nothing, or for something that others thought I did (not good). My brother has a female friend who was accused of bearing a child by a man other than her husband. There wasn't a shred of truth in the finger-pointing, but the false accusation rapidly took on a life of its own. Her husband was ready to get a DNA test and then sue the miscreant, but their pastor told them they should not be held hostage by a lie. Recently the accused woman told my brother that the situation brought her to one of the lowest points of her life, even though she'd done absolutely nothing wrong and was perfectly innocent.

Are you at peace with God and with yourself? Ever wonder if God still loves you? Let's say, for example, you have a bad habit . . . an addiction . . . an attitude. Or you just had a huge family fight last night . . . you said terrible things to one another . . . you used profanity. And now you're reading this book, and God is speaking to your heart.

Do you feel badly? Should you ever feel badly?

Guilt and shame are complex and powerful human experiences. While sometimes I feel shame for no reason, other times, when I really am guilty, I feel little or no remorse unless I'm found out! If we *are* forgiven, though—if God has taken our sins away from us forever, and there is no condemnation for those who are in Christ Jesus—then *why* do we still feel guilty? *Should* we feel guilty? Should we feel guilty that we feel guilty? Or should we just be angry at the church, at preachers, at religious people for making us feel guilty? After all, when you leave church, you want to feel good about yourself, right?

Shame can be suffocating, and apart from Christ's sacrifice I'm left to deal with shame on my own. I have three options: blame and shame others, shame myself, or give my shame to Christ. Let's look at each of these.

First, *I can deny my sin and perhaps somehow blame someone else for what I did.* Denial and blaming others go hand in hand. Listen to Adam and Eve right after they ate the forbidden fruit:

> The man said, "The woman you put here with me—she gave
> me some fruit from the tree, and I ate it." Then the LORD
> God said to the woman, "What is this you have done?" The
> woman said, "The serpent deceived me, and I ate."
>
> GENESIS 3:12–13

Studies have found that, generally, when people *themselves* do something wrong, they tend to use their circumstances to excuse their behavior; however, when they see *somebody else* doing something wrong, they are quick to attribute it to a character flaw. If I do something stupid, well, I just couldn't help myself this time—forgive me and get over it. But if you do something I don't like, you're a bad person without excuse, and you'll be fortunate if I can find it in my heart to forgive you.

If you don't think every one of us is baptized in denial, think back to the last time you drove your car and did something dumb. Mine was yesterday, driving up to the retreat center to write this book. The left arrow turned green, and I shot into the intersection. Only, I wasn't in the left-turn lane. For me, the light was still red, but I was so far out when I realized my mistake, I just kept going.

The guy making an oncoming left turn wasn't real happy. I heard a long horn blast, and I think he was waving at me. But hey, I was talking to my son on my cell phone! He just told me that he and his wife are going to have a boy! The guy in the other truck should under-stand that! And I'm normally a good driver, anyway!

So somehow I convince myself that I am not really sinful, or I'm not *that* sinful. Or maybe there is no such things as sin. This, of course, is the principal doctrine of popular unreligion: There is no such thing as absolute truth. Our world has come to the conclusion that nothing is *absolutely* right or wrong, and God have mercy if we suggest in our public institutions that people have a sin problem.

We can barely talk about sin in church anymore, let alone in office spaces and university classrooms. People scoff at the "idea" of sin and remind us that teaching about our fallenness only makes people feel bad about themselves. That's the real downside of religion, unreligious people tell us religiously. In other words, people having problems doesn't mean those "problems" are related to sin . . . which brings us to the next way to deal with guilt and shame.

Second, *I can try to fix the problem through my own efforts.* When Adam and Eve realized they were naked, they felt shame. Instead of turning to God for forgiveness and transformation, though, "they sewed fig leaves together and made coverings for themselves."[4] To me, penance (broadly) is simply my attempt to make up for or cover over my sins. To try to alleviate my guilt and shame. Something. Anything. It's the pain of sin, the weight of the evil in all of us: "My guilt has overwhelmed me like a burden too heavy to bear."[5]

What to do?

Third, *I can turn to Christ to be set free from shame:*

He was pierced for our transgressions,
he was crushed for our iniquities;

the punishment that brought us peace was upon him,
and by his wounds we are healed.

ISAIAH 53:5

The irony, indeed, the deception, is that people think *God* shames them, so, like Adam and Eve, they hide. No doubt, there's a lot of negative stuff in organized religion, and simple people who need God are sometimes abused by self-righteous leaders. *Jesus isn't like that.* To a sea of sad faces burdened with life and unreasonable religious expectations, he said,

Come to me, all you who are weary and burdened, and I will
give you rest. Take my yoke upon you and learn from me, for
I am gentle and humble in heart, and you will find rest for
your souls. For my yoke is easy and my burden is light.

MATTHEW 11:28–30

GUILT-FREE LIVING

The Bible, particularly the tenth chapter of the letter to the Hebrews, answers some of these questions. As we return to Hebrews 10, I again recommend that you stop here and read through it. This passage explains how the sacrifice of Christ is more than enough to cover all of your sins and, practically speaking, how that should change the way you perceive yourself too—how to get past your past by forgiving yourself. Let's go through this step by step.

First, *you have to understand and accept the perfect, finished work of Christ.* Yes, we're back to this: Experiencing perfect freedom from your sin can only happen when you understand that from God's perspective you are perfect. Anything less than perfection will give us the sense of falling short, but with the righteousness of Christ in us, we measure up perfectly to God's standards. Remember this?

Day after day every [old covenant] priest stands and performs
his religious duties; again and again he offers the same sacrifices [penance], which can never take away sins. "But when
this priest [Christ Jesus] had offered for all time one sacrifice
for sins, he sat down at the right hand of God. Since that

time he waits for his enemies to be made his footstool,
because by one sacrifice he has made perfect forever those
who are being made holy.

HEBREWS 10:11–14

Not only has Christ's sacrifice made you perfect, it's made you perfect forever.

SELF-IMPOSED AMNESIA

The Holy Spirit also testifies to us about this. First he says:
"This is the covenant I will make with them after that time,
says the Lord. I will put my laws in their hearts, and I will
write them on their minds." Then he adds: "Their sins and
lawless acts *I will remember no more.*"

HEBREWS 10:15–17, EMPHASIS MINE

Again: God accepts you so unconditionally that when he sees you,
it's as if you never sinned against him. *Once you've been forgiven, your
sins are gone!*

Picture the people who've hurt you: The guy in the other car who's
sneering and making obscene gestures . . . the ex who cheated and
lied . . . the school bully who spit in your face . . . the friend who
stabbed you in the back with vicious gossip. Now try to imagine a
world where no one, when looking into the face of the one who caused
them pain, can remember what was said or done. When Jesus is in
you and you are forgiven, God looks at your face and refuses to
remember what you did to sin against him.

Humans naturally know nothing of this unconditional grace, and
world religions know nothing of this comprehensive, no-strings-
attached God-forgiveness, but it's the pillar of the new covenant in
Christ's blood,[6] God forgets because forgiveness is self-imposed amne-
sia. It's not that he can't recall the facts of your life, good and bad, but
if and when he does think of your *sins,* it is totally and completely
without any effect on how he thinks of *you.*

We can't imagine such forgiveness because loving our enemies,
truly caring for those who hate us, is humanly inconceivable. So we
think *God* can't love like that, because *we* can't love like that. But we

must not water down God's love based on our bad ideas of love. Instead, we need to let God's inconceivably perfect love transform the way we love—it is, after all, *his* love within us. "To forgive sins," wrote Kierkegaard, "is divine not only in the sense that no one is able to do it except God, but also because no one can do it without God."[7]

> You rest in the forgiveness of sin when the thought of God does not remind you of the sin but that it is forgiven, when the past is not a memory of how much you trespassed but of how much you have been forgiven.
> —Søren Kierkegaard

The writer of Hebrews goes on to say, "Where these [our sins and lawless acts] have been forgiven, there is no longer any sacrifice for sin."[8] In other words, a perfect sacrifice is just that: perfect. Nothing else is necessary. To say that all your sins are not totally forgiven, after God has forgiven them, is a backhanded way of saying that Christ's sacrifice was *not* perfect and was not enough! Jesus did *not* say on the cross, "It is mostly finished, nearly perfect—the rest is up to you."[9]

Certainly sin still has its consequences: We will reap whatever we sow.[10] A convicted murderer, for example, isn't necessarily paroled just because he becomes born again, and his feelings of remorse may not go away either. Nonetheless, the worst imaginable consequence of sin—separation from God forever—*is* taken away, *forever*. Never again will any sin sever us from God.[11]

If feeling badly about yourself is a step toward personal change, then great! This is what we Christ-followers call *conviction,* those tense moments of divine provocation that make us aware of our actual guilt. In fact, it's a serious problem if you never feel badly about what you do. If, however, feeling badly about yourself is an obsession, and it doesn't lead to positive change, then that's a problem too! Unremitting guilt is from the devil, not from God.

HURTING FOR GOD

Some years ago, right here at this retreat center, I had a profound God-experience unlike any other before or since. Though I came to work, not to pray, my life was in crisis, so for the next two days I prayed and did very little work. It was one of the few times I can say that Jesus "appeared" to me, primarily to confront me about unresolved relationship issues.

Years earlier I'd been diagnosed with an incurable heart disease, cardiomyopathy,[12] but God *still* didn't have my full attention. Somehow, though, on this bright, sunny day in Central Arizona's lovely Verde Valley, something happened to me that I'm not fully able to explain. It wasn't quite like the apostle Paul's out-of-the-body road trip,[13] but it was transformational. Most remarkably, as my life passed before me, as I saw the faces of people whom I'd caused pain, I felt with equal measure both "the goodness and severity"[14] of God. He spoke to me directly and deeply about changes I needed to make in my life, but I never for a moment felt rejection or shame. He was firm without being harsh, full of grace without tolerating my sin, convicting but not condemning.

The conviction of the Holy Spirit always comes packaged in the *comfort* of God's love and acceptance, the *hope* that you can and will change, and the *power* to make it happen. The Bible calls the Spirit "another counselor,"[15] from a Greek term that means "someone who comes alongside you to defend, but not a lawyer, a friend."[16] The word carries with it the idea of correction and comfort in equal amounts. God speaks "the truth in love."[17]

On the other hand, the devil's condemnation always comes packaged with a sense of God's rejection, the hopeless feeling that your life will probably never change, the subliminal sense that God is giving up on you, and the futile helplessness of it all. Rejection, hopelessness, helplessness—the Holy Spirit is *never* any of those things.

HOW TO EXPERIENCE GOD'S FORGIVENESS

There's a huge difference between (1) the fact of God's unconditional forgiveness and (2) whether you and I actually know and experience his love. It's one thing to be saved by grace, it's another to *know* you're saved by grace, to know beyond a shadow of a doubt that you have eternal life. For that to happen, you must ask for God's forgiveness.

King David was a bad boy. Standing on his rooftop one sleepless evening, he saw below him a woman bathing next door. "The woman was very beautiful, and David sent someone to find out about her. The man said, 'Isn't this Bathsheba . . . *the wife of Uriah the Hittite?*' "[18] But David sent for her anyway, slept with her, and they conceived. When he found out she was expecting, he sent away for her husband, Uriah, who was off to war for Israel.

> The grace of being chosen and loved by God counts more than betrayal.
> —Ray Anderson, *The Gospel According to Judas*

Hoping Uriah would do his manly duty, David figured that his own adulterous affair would go undetected. Much to David's dismay, though, Uriah refused to sleep with his wife. This man of unusual honor indignantly replied, "How can I share a bed with my woman when my brothers are out there sleeping in tents and risking their lives for their country?"[19] So David sent Uriah back to war with a sealed order for his commanding officer to lead him into the heat of the battle, then withdraw, leaving him to die.

King David did this. A man of God did this. And then he said nothing, bottling up his guilt until his personal chaplain, the prophet Nathan, confronted him about his sin. David wrote,

> Blessed is the man whose sin the LORD does not count against him and in whose spirit is no deceit. When I kept silent, my bones wasted away through my groaning all day long. For day and night your hand was heavy upon me; my strength was sapped as in the heat of summer. . . . Then I acknowledged my sin to you and did not cover up my iniquity. I said, "I will confess my transgressions to the LORD"— and you forgave the *guilt* of my sin.
>
> PSALM 32:2–5, EMPHASIS MINE

When I confess my sins to God, he takes away the *guilt* of my sin. Guilt (in the sense of persistent shame) stands between me and the *experience* of his forgiveness, that is, even though I know God forgives all, I don't *feel* it, don't sense it, don't live freely in his forgiveness. Yes, guilt (conviction) turns me toward God; it's the Holy Spirit reminding me that not only am I God's child. In contrast, condemnation and shame are from the devil, who wants me to doubt that I'm a child of God, to wonder if God still loves me. Shame (condemnation) is the devil trying to convince me that I am not God's child.

Here's the point: God doesn't want you to change so he can *accept* you. No, he wants you to confess your sin—to admit it to him and to yourself—so he can *change* you. John writes, "If we claim to be without sin, we deceive ourselves and the truth is not in us. If we confess our sins, he is faithful and just and will forgive us our sins and purify us from all unrighteousness."[20]

PASSTHROUGH

Back to Hebrews 10. Christ's sacrifice is more than enough to cover all your sins, and, practically speaking, that should change your perspective and experience about God and yourself. Remember: First, *you have to understand and accept the perfect, finished work of Christ.*

Second, *you have to believe what you know and understand.* You have to choose confidence. Faith is the evidence of what you don't see, and it's also the assurance of what you might not feel. God says you are forgiven; when your feelings tell you otherwise, what are you going to believe? God or your feelings?

> Therefore, brothers, [because of what Christ has done,
> because his perfect sacrifice has made you perfect in the sight
> of a perfect God,] *we have confidence* to enter the Most Holy
> Place by the blood of Jesus, by a new and living way opened
> for us through the curtain, that is, his body, and since we
> have a great priest over the house of God, let us draw near to
> God with a sincere heart *in full assurance of faith,* having our
> hearts sprinkled to cleanse us from a guilty conscience and
> having our bodies washed with pure water.
>
> HEBREWS 10:19–22, EMPHASIS MINE

The moment Christ died on the cross, the earth shook, the sky darkened. Suddenly, the thick fabric-draped entrance to the Holy of Holies—"the veil" in the temple—was shredded violently from top to bottom. For centuries that place had been so sacred that only the high priest could go behind that curtain . . . and only once a year on the Day of Atonement (Yom Kippur) . . . and only with a bowl of blood.[21]

When Christ died, all of this changed forever. His consummate sacrifice meant the end of animal sacrifices, forever. It also meant that now, all of us, any of us, can enter directly into the holy presence of the perfect God: "We have confidence to enter the Most Holy Place by the blood of Jesus, by a new and living way opened for us through the curtain, that is, his body."[22]

Amazing! That curtain was a symbol of Christ himself; to enter God's transforming presence, we pass through Christ! In other words, Jesus isn't someone we merely believe *in;* when we come to the Cross and believe *into* him, we are joined in mystical union as we pass through his torn body into God's presence. When we come to the Cross, we *experience* God's presence and power—not just as an emotional experience, but as a genuine encounter. As I enter God's reality, *the* reality, his reality changes mine.

> God will keep his promises, even if it kills him.

I've already explained the difference between believing *in* and believing *into,* but let me reinforce it here. Relationship with God is not just a matter of the mind, believing *in* God, accepting the facts of Christ's work as truth. Yes, that's a starting point, and yes, we must give wholehearted assent to the Bible and what it tells us about the Savior's death and resurrection. But remember, the Greek term *alétheia,* translated *truth,* means "reality," and coming to Christ—believing *into* him—is a transformational encounter with the reality of God. Believing there is true life outside the matrix is one thing; taking the red pill and getting out of the illusion is another!

The bloody body of Jesus, so vividly portrayed in *The Passion of the Christ,* is an entry point, a passage into the love and forgiveness of a holy God. His shredded body is the only exit from the matrix of sin, guilt, and death.

A CARCASS, A CURTAIN, A CROSS

This takes us back to what has to be one of the most mysterious events of the Old Testament.[23] God appeared to Abram (later to be renamed Abraham) and promised him descendants as numerous as the stars. Then, to seal his promise, God instructed Abram to bring him a goat, a ram, a dove, and a young pigeon. Abram cut the larger animals in half and laid the split carcasses on the ground. In a fairly common practice in an ancient world where paper documents didn't exist, two people would walk together, side by side, between the two halves of a carcass and vow, "May what has happened to this animal happen to me if I do not keep my oath." In fact, the Hebrew word for *covenant*[24] means literally "to cut."

Who needs lawyers!

I've had half a notion to introduce this idea into wedding cere-monies at our church. People take marriage commitment too lightly these days. Can't you just see the bride and groom walking between two bloody halves of a goat as they exit?

Sorry.

Abram sat there waiting for God to do something . . . say some-thing. Only the whoosh of predatory birds descending on the carcasses broke the desert silence. Abram chased them away.

The day wore on.

And then suddenly, "when the sun had set and darkness had fallen, a smoking firepot with a blazing torch appeared and passed between the pieces." While Abram watched passively, *God passed between the two halves of the carcasses!* "On that day the LORD made a covenant [literally, "cut a covenant"] with Abram."[25]

Right now my heart is *pounding* with zeal and dread as I recount this incredible story and consider how these images are fulfilled in Christ on the cross! God, in effect, was saying, "I will bring you into the land of promise, I will bless you, and your people will be my peo-ple, *even if it kills me.*"

And it did.

God will keep his covenant over his own dead body, and we are reminded of this every time we celebrate Holy Communion: "This is my body given for you."[26]

Just as Jews celebrate Pass*over*,[27] maybe on Good Friday we Christ-followers should be celebrating Pass*through*!

Furthermore, God passed through the split carcasses *alone*—not side by side with Abram, as would fit tradition—which indicated he was taking full and unilateral responsibility to ensure that his promises were fulfilled. This is a dramatic picture of grace, God's one-sided initiative to save us through the rending of his Son's body.[28]

That "we have confidence to enter the Most Holy Place by the blood of Jesus . . . through the curtain, that is, his body" means that we enter into permanent covenant relationship with God, not based on what we have done but on God's oath, his promise bound by the death of his own Son.

> When God made his promise to Abraham, since there was no one greater for him to swear by, he swore by himself, saying, "I will surely bless you and give you many descendants." And so after waiting patiently, Abraham received what was promised.
>
> Men swear by someone greater than themselves, and the oath confirms what is said and puts an end to all argument. Because God wanted to make the unchanging nature of his purpose very clear to the heirs of what was promised, he confirmed it with an oath. God did this so that, by two unchangeable things in which it is impossible for God to lie, we who have fled to take hold of the hope offered to us may be greatly encouraged.
>
> We have this hope as an anchor for the soul, firm and secure. It enters the inner sanctuary behind the curtain, where Jesus, who went before us, has entered on our behalf.
>
> HEBREWS 6:13–20

Third, *you have to hold on to this faith*. Faith for the moment, day after day, is faithfulness: "Let us hold unswervingly to the hope we profess, for he who promised is faithful."[29] This needs little explanation and a lot of application.

Fourth, *you have to live it out:* "Let us consider how we may spur one another on toward love and good deeds."[30] Why would we need to "spur one another on" if we're perfect? It's the simple difference between already being saved and working out your salvation.[31] I especially like the word *spur,* which is not *exactly* the meaning of the Greek term but it's close. The verb form means "to provoke, to irritate." It's an edgy word, and the lesson I draw is that God uses edgy, imperfect people who from his point of view are already perfect. I'm so grateful that even though I live in the present, God lives in eternity, and that from his perspective his plan for my life is already realized. I'm not stuck in my past—I'm bound to God's absolutely certain future.

Doing good, then, is a practical way to becoming good, to growing into what God plans for us, "for we are God's workmanship, created in Christ Jesus to do good works, which God prepared in advance for us to do."[32] There is transformational power in doing what's right, even if you're doing what's right for no other reason than that you have to. It's better, though, to do right because you want to, and it's best to do right without even thinking about it because it's just part of you. Loving others will help you stop hating yourself.

Fifth, you have to keep talking about it: "Let us not give up meeting together, as some are in the habit of doing, but let us encourage one another—and all the more as you see the Day approaching."[33] We can't provoke one another, spur one another on to good works, if we don't see each other. As a pastor, I'm often troubled by the marginal influence the Christian community has on those who are a part of that community. In fact, I'm not sure it's even appropriate to refer to the church as a Christian "community," because often people are so lonely and alone.

Recently a friend—pained and shamed—announced to a group of us that his unmarried daughter was pregnant. He was very angry, too. To his amazement, none of us affirmed his shame, and all of us re-affirmed God's love, acceptance, forgiveness. *We need one another,* because we cannot fully experience the forgiveness of sins and release from shame alone.

Sixth, and finally, *you have to* (and here's a Greek word for you) *fuhgeddabahdit,* which means, "forget about it!" If God doesn't hold our sins against us, then what are we doing to ourselves by going where he doesn't go?

> I do not consider myself yet to have taken hold of [everything God has for me.] But one thing I do: *Forgetting what is behind* and straining toward what is ahead, I press on toward the goal to win the prize for which God has called me heavenward in Christ Jesus.
>
> PHILIPPIANS 3:13–14, EMPHASIS MINE

Paul didn't mean that your past is out of sight, out of mind, but that when you think about it, you don't let the memory affect your forward progress. Hold on to the promises of God, and when you do, the past won't be able to hold on to you.

When the Bible tells us to remember something, it means we are to remember it for life-changing reasons. On the other hand, when the Bible tells us to forget about something, it doesn't mean that everything you remember will vanish from your brain as though you have spiritual Alzheimer's. It means you forget in the sense that when you do think about it, you refuse to let it hold you back. *If God forgets your sins, then you should too!*

Viewpoint #2:
The Cross is the exit door from sin's pain: guilt and shame.

SCRIPTURE

†2M "Since we have confidence to enter the Most Holy Place by the blood of Jesus, by a new and living way opened for us through the curtain, that is, his body, and since we have a great priest over the house of God, let us draw near to God with a sincere heart in full assurance of faith, having our hearts sprinkled to cleanse us from a guilty conscience."[34]

†2Tu "Then I acknowledged my sin to you and did not cover up my iniquity. I said, 'I will confess my transgressions to the LORD'—and you forgave the guilt of my sin."[35]

†2W "The [Old Testament] gifts and sacrifices being offered were not able to clear the conscience of the worshiper. They are only a matter of food and drink and various ceremonial washings—external regulations applying until the time of the new order. . . .

"How much more, then, will the blood of Christ, who through the eternal Spirit offered himself unblemished to God, cleanse our consciences from acts that lead to death, so that we may serve the living God!"[36]

†2Th "In him we have redemption through his blood, the forgiveness of sins, in accordance with the riches of God's grace that
he lavished on us with all wisdom and understanding."[37]

†2F "'Father, forgive them, for they do not know what they are
doing.'"[38]

†2Sa "Now he [God] has reconciled you by Christ's physical body
through death to present you holy in his sight, without blem-
ish and free from accusation."[39]

†2Su "There is now no condemnation for those who are in Christ
Jesus."[40]

CHAPTER SEVEN

Slaves

Viewpoint #3:
The Cross is an exit door from the power of habitual sin.

You are a slave, Neo. Like everyone else you were born into bondage, born into a prison.
    —Morpheus

Like gravity, hypocrisy, and the perils of 3D . . .
    and thinking so much differently
So pardon me while I burst into flames.
I've had enough of this world,
    and its people's mindless games.
    —Brandon Boyd, lead singer of *Incubus*

At one time we too were foolish, disobedient, deceived and
enslaved by all kinds of passions and pleasures. We lived in malice
and envy, being hated and hating one another.
    —Titus 3:3

I'm struggling.

No, I'm not having writer's block. I'm trying to manage my tortured soul. I don't feel like writing this chapter, or even the rest of this book, because last night I had a crisis. At least that's the reason I gave the people at the retreat center for getting here a day late.

I was due to arrive last night. My plan was to leave after work, make the two-hour drive, get a good night's sleep, and start writing early this morning. It didn't work out that way, because at the end of a long day, my wife and I had a serious disagreement over . . . well . . . I can't really explain it to you. We couldn't really explain it to each other. Oh, there was some little thing that started the whole mess, but mostly we found ourselves stuck in the same patterns of misunderstanding we've had off and on for years. Same old, same old. Civil war.

No, our marriage isn't at risk—never has been. Even so, anyone who's been married for, let's say, longer than a honeymoon, will discover that certain situations can trigger a sequence of dysfunctional responses that make us feel helpless. Feel powerless. Feel like hell.

Now here I am, much later in the day, sitting in front of my laptop, confessing to you my personal sin and pain. The good news is that Marilyn and I resolved our misunderstandings before I left. Well . . . at least I prayed some . . . we prayed together . . . and we told each other we were sorry. But it's taking me a while to get over it. Not her. It. Me. My recurring inability to be Christlike.

Last night, while I was so upset, I kept thinking to myself, *Tomorrow and the rest of this week I'm going to be writing about the Cross, but right now, I'm so far away from what I hope to write that I have no hope.*

And then I realized, just moments ago, that what I'm feeling is exactly what I need to write about in this chapter: enslavement.

> I know that nothing good lives in me, that is, in my sinful nature. For I have the desire to do what is good, but I cannot carry it out. For what I do is not the good I want to do; no, the evil I do not want to do—this I keep on doing. . . . What a wretched man I am! Who will rescue me from this body of death?
>
> ROMANS 7:18–19, 24

Yes, the apostle Paul wrote that, and he wasn't looking back at his pre-Christian life. He was speaking as a man who knew and loved God but hated things about himself, things over which he seemed to have little or no control. Frankly, I'm grateful for Paul's candid self-disclosure. He's not an excuse for my personal failings, but reading what he has to say about human nature, about himself, makes me realize that I'm not alone in the struggle.

New Testament scholar F. F. Bruce wrote of Paul,

> Some writers have no doubt used the letter-form to conceal their true thoughts; Paul's transparent honesty was incompatible with any such artificiality. He tries, where necessary, to be diplomatic, whether he is writing to his own converts or to people personally unknown to him; but even so he wears his heart on his sleeve.[1]

In the last chapter, I explained how the Cross sets us free from the guilt and shame of sin. In this chapter, I want to help you understand how the Cross sets us free from the power and enslavement of sin.

CIVIL WAR

I'm hugely interested in military history, particularly the American Civil War.[2] I've visited nearly every major battlefield in Pennsylvania, Maryland, Virginia, Georgia, South Carolina, Tennessee, and Missouri. Last year my wife and I and some close friends traveled back to western Maryland to watch the 140-year anniversary reenactment of the Battle of Antietam. Outfitted precisely as soldiers were in the war, *fifteen thousand* reenactors participated in a stunning spectacle of living history.

Flashing, thundering cannon broke the predawn silence, and battle flags rippled as tidy ranks of thousands marched toward one another across an open field. Within minutes, the scene before us melted into a thick haze from the sparkling muzzles of ten thousand black-powder guns. One of our friends standing behind me said, "War is insane." Northern General William T. Sherman said it was hell.

The Civil War, as you well know, was a war for the Union. At least that's how it began, as a conflict over states' rights, over how much power the central (federal) government could exercise over places like South Carolina and Texas. In rebellion against what was perceived as an increasingly oppressive federal government, southern states began to withdraw from the Union and form their own government, which they called the Confederate States of America.

Our president, Abraham Lincoln, who was under pressure from abolitionists like Henry Ward Beecher to make the war a fight against the abomination of human slavery, responded (and this surprises many), "If by keeping slavery I could preserve the Union, I would keep slavery, and if by abolishing slavery I could save the Union, I would abolish slavery." After two bloody years of conflict, though, it became more and more evident that the North needed a moral cause. In some ways, Lincoln was backed into the decision to emancipate the millions of Africans who had been forcibly relocated from their peaceful villages to work the sweltering cotton fields of the American South.

Because slaves cannot buy their own freedom, someone on the outside of the slave market has to purchase it for them. American slaves were redeemed by the blood of six hundred thousand American soldiers, thousands of them black. More died in the Civil War than in all the other American wars combined—a full 5 percent of the American population at the time. Imagine the toll: Today, 5 percent of the U.S. would be nearly thirty million people! At Antietam, in just a couple of morning hours, more men died in the forty-acre Cornfield than at the beaches of Normandy on World War II's D-Day. And the battle had only begun—before the day was over, 23,000 men were killed, wounded, or missing.

The reenactment of that battle, The Cornfield, was done offsite, because the national battlefield park is sacred ground. That's precisely how my friend Wayne felt as he stood atop a stone wall overlooking the cornfield of lost dreams. He whispered, "This is a religious experience. Just to think about how many men sacrificed their lives in this place."

Most Americans have heard of Gettysburg (in my spell-check), where fifty thousand were lost in three days. Few know of Antietam (*not* in my spell-check), which led directly to Abraham Lincoln's decision to free the slaves by issuing the now immortal Emancipation

Proclamation of 1863. You can read about this, and the battle of Antietam, on the Lincoln Memorial in Washington, D.C., where one hundred years later, Dr. Martin Luther King Jr. told the world, "I have a dream."

Woven into the fabric of the American soul are the words of the "Battle Hymn of the Republic," written during the Civil War:

> In the beauty of the lilies Christ was born across the sea,
> With a glory in his bosom that transfigures you and me.
> As he died to make men holy,
> *Let us die to make men free.*[3]

REBELS AND SLAVES

Jesus died to make us free. Jesus died to emancipate us from the slavery of sin. Not only do I need to be forgiven, released from sin's penalty and pain, I need to be delivered from its power, an ugly over-lord that, now and then, reawakens in me and makes me forget I'm under another Master. Like last night when I was so angry with my wife.

Here's how Paul described the problem:

> If the power of sin within me keeps sabotaging my best intentions, I obviously need help! I realize that I don't have what it takes. I can will it, but I can't do it. I decide to do good, but I don't really do it; I decide not to do bad, but then I do it anyway. My decisions, such as they are, don't result in actions. Something has gone wrong deep within me and gets the better of me every time.
>
> It happens so regularly that it's predictable. The moment I decide to do good, sin is there to trip me up. I truly delight in God's commands, but it's pretty obvious that not all of me joins in that delight. Parts of me covertly rebel, and just when I least expect it, they take charge. I've tried everything and nothing helps. I'm at the end of my rope. Is there no one who can do anything for me? Isn't that the real question?
>
> ROMANS 7:17–24 THE MESSAGE

Even when I receive God's forgiveness for my sins, even when I know that God, in Christ, has forgiven me fully and unconditionally, the beat goes on. I still sin. What's up with that? I suppose it's not unlike freeing the nineteenth-century slaves. When Abraham Lincoln issued the Emancipation Proclamation, virtually nothing changed. Until the North won the war after shedding rivers of blood, one of the great documents of American history was just another piece of paper.

Even after the war ended, most African-Americans languished for decades in the slavery of imaginary freedom. People of color waited another one hundred years before their civil rights *began* to be restored to them. Being free doesn't necessarily mean a person can or will live freely. While no slave can live in freedom, emancipated slaves can still live in the powerful shadow of their past.

LITTLE BIRDS AND STEAK IN THE MATRIX

Years ago we had a bright blue parakeet. Poor little fella. We fed him daily, and he was never without water, but we rarely handled this sweet little creature. When on occasion I took him out of his cage, his soft, scratchy, cold little bird feet would clutch my index finger, and like the needle of a compass obsessed with *North,* no matter which way I held him, he'd stretch his little head back toward the safety of his cage.

Noticing his eyes bulging toward his private prison, I had to think about how we can be bound to habits, enslaved by the past. Imagine a bird desperately wanting to go back into a cage—that's not how God created birds! Imagine the Israelites, not long free from their slavery in Egypt, wanting to go back there! They missed eating fish. And onions and garlic. And leeks? Who would miss *that*?! But if that's what you're used to, forget about the milk and honey of the Promised Land.[4]

Reminds me of Cypher, the Judas figure in *The Matrix.* Cypher's free from the Matrix, and he knows what real reality is, but because life is difficult in the real world, he longs for the "safe" illusion of the Matrix, especially the sensual delight of a steak dinner. Everything in the Matrix is imagined, but Cypher's memory of his former life seduces him, like a man being reintroduced to heroin. Ultimately, he betrays Morpheus and Neo in exchange for being returned to the enslavement of suspended animation.

Did you ever work for somebody you couldn't stand? Remember how that person was *so* controlling? Or maybe it was your mother or your father. Earlier I told you about my surly boss who made me clean up a nasty mess. *Years* later I was shopping with my wife, and there he was, still selling furniture. When I saw his face, I turned away, making no effort to say hello.

Even though God had worked dramatically in my life through that man's difficult personality, I found myself emotionally immobilized by my old master. As another example, to this day my own children cringe when I speak to them with a certain tone of voice, and I have to admit that sometimes I take strange pleasure in annoying them this way. My mother, who turns eighty next year, still irks me . . . and I still hear my father's deep voice. He's been gone for a few years, but I have his table saw, and whenever I use it, I think about him . . . and how fussy he was about his power tools.

A couple of years ago I set a bag of oranges on top of the saw. And forgot about 'em, only to discover a few days later that the bag had leaked. There on the steel top of my *dad's* table saw, in *my* garage, was an ugly rust stain. My first thought (honestly) was, *Oh no, Dad isn't going to like this at all—he's gonna kill me! I should never have borrowed his saw.*

Oops.

"It's *my* table saw now," I told myself, and for a moment I thought I caught a glimpse of my dad standing there with Jesus, smiling . . . laughing. So grabbing a fist full of steel wool, I quickly scrubbed the table saw clean.*

PHONE BOOTHS TO FREEDOM

A megaphone for howling devils, your old nature is no different. For instance, as much as you must always honor your father and mother (it's the fourth commandment, you know), once you leave home, you don't have to *obey* them. In a similar way, you need to remind both your old nature and the devil that you are, as Paul wrote, "dead to sin but alive to God."[5]

---

*No, I didn't actually see my dad with Jesus, but I did feel compelled to clean the top as soon as possible!

I'd like to offer some practical advice on how to manage the old master. You're not his slave anymore. He's yours because of what Jesus did on the cross. So what are you going to do about it? "Advice" probably isn't a helpful term—that sounds like something you *should* do. Instead, think of these practical steps as exit doors from the matrix of your past and entrance doors to the life you've always wanted. To me, the more I walk with God, the more I realize that every moment of obedience, every moment of reflection offers an opportunity for transformational encounter. In a very real sense, what follows are power points, steps closer into the presence of God.

First, *remind yourself you are not alone. Everyone* has a problem with recurring sin, and anyone who tells you otherwise is fooling himself. Stop the self-righteous pretending. This is why the life of Paul encourages me so deeply: Jesus is my Lord and Savior, but Paul is my hero, because I see him struggling with all the things that seem so difficult for me . . . and I see him finding God's grace to sustain him. Paul could never fully escape certain elements of his fallenness, but he learned to live with himself and above himself.

As a therapist might describe it, Paul learned how to manage himself, like this: "In your anger do not sin: Do not let the sun go down while you are still angry."[6] In other words, being a Christ-follower doesn't mean your emotions, or even your weaknesses, will go away: "For Christ's sake, I delight in weaknesses, in insults, in hardships, in persecutions, in difficulties. For when I am weak, then I am strong."[7]

Shall we go on sinning so that grace may increase? Of course not![8] But again, "if we claim to be without sin, we deceive ourselves and the truth is not in us."[9] In the Greek text of this verse, the tense is present-linear; that is, it expresses *continuous, uninterrupted action.*[10] Thus, for the Christian, confession of sin is not something we do intermittently every few days or weeks: *It's a way of life,* an ongoing exercise of openness with God, agreeing with him moment by moment that we need his cleansing and grace.

Second, *believe you are dead to sin, and live like it.* Say no to the matrix. Say no to the illusion. Live like Rosa Parks, an ordinary woman who became a hero to millions. Rosa Parks was the black woman who one day decided she was not going to sit in the back of the bus just because of her skin color. A day just like any other became a day of deliverance, a day of freedom, when one little woman stood up to oppression. It was her right.

Even though so many of her people still lived in the illusion of enslavement, Rosa Parks decided it was time for that to end. The Emancipation Proclamation was a century old, and though no one owned slaves, some people were still living like chattel. Standing up against the subjugation of the black and white matrix, Rosa Parks sat herself down once and for all in the pages of American justice and freedom.

Stand up to your old nature, your old slave-master:

> Count yourselves dead to sin but alive to God in Christ Jesus. Therefore do not let sin reign in your mortal body so that you obey its evil desires. Do not offer the parts of your body to sin, as instruments of wickedness, but rather offer your- selves to God, as those who have been brought from death to life; and offer the parts of your body to him as instruments of righteousness.
>
> ROMANS 6:11–13

In Eugene Peterson's paraphrase:

> You must not give sin a vote in the way you conduct your lives. Don't give it the time of day. Don't even run little errands that are connected with that old way of life. Throw yourselves wholeheartedly and full-time—remember, you've been raised from the dead!—into God's way of doing things. Sin can't tell you how to live. After all, you're not living under that old tyranny any longer. You're living in the freedom of God.[11]

Third, *confess your failures to God . . . and to someone you trust.* It's totally true: honesty is the best policy. You don't have to tell everybody everything about your life, but you'd better tell God. Of course, he already knows everything about you, but honesty with him enacts something extraordinarily liberating inside of you: "If we confess our sins, he is faithful and just and will forgive us our sins *and purify us from all unrighteousness.*"[12]

This verse, in the original Greek, is also in the present-linear tense, which means that we must *keep on* confessing our sins. We don't do this in some morbid reliving of the past, as in telling God over and over how sorry we are for something we did once. We keep on confessing, though, when we repeatedly commit the same old sins.

Even though I am crucified with Christ; even though my fallen nature has been put to death on the Cross, until the day I die, that old self of mine is going to keep trying to stay alive. It keeps coming back like an old disco tune. You hate that kind of music, but it just sticks in your head:

Stayin' alive, stayin' alive.

Like Paul, every day I think and do things I shouldn't . . . and don't think and do things I should. On the way to the retreat center, while I was angry with myself for getting angry with my dear wife, I got angry with someone who raced ahead of me on the freeway entrance ramp.

Who shall deliver me from this body of death?

Thank God, his mercies are new every morning.[13] For me, they're new every hour! When I confess my sins to God, when I agree with him about my sin, he is faithful to forgive me and to keep purging my life of self-destructive behaviors. In other words, *confession of sin is transformational.*

Just about any therapist will affirm that denial and avoidance behaviors are, perhaps, the crux of human dysfunction. M. Scott Peck, a psychiatrist and bestselling author, who wrote one of his lesser-known books about denial as the root of human evil,[14] concluded that mental health is relentless dedication to reality at all costs, while people who are mentally ill are those unable or unwilling to see life as it actually is.

I've said it this way: Mental health is the ability to think about what you think. Those on the upper end of the dysfunctional curve seem to lack the ability to be straightforward with themselves. A couple of years ago at the Willow Creek Leadership Summit, one speaker said, "The more a leader [or anyone] needs to change, the less the leader knows [he or she] needs to change."

Confession is a phone booth, a place to run in order to flee the matrix of darkness and to enter the world of God's light. Confession gets us right with God, lines us up with the real world, and cleans us out inside. Without an essential willingness to look at ourselves honestly and take unwavering responsibility for our thoughts, attitudes, and behaviors, there's little hope for our future or for the future of the relationships we cherish.

WHAT PROTESTANTS CAN LEARN FROM CATHOLICS

Confession is a sacrament. In the Catholic communion, it's one of seven "official" sacraments.[15] I understand this somewhat because I was baptized, raised, and confirmed a Lutheran. As a young man, I learned about the "means of grace," that the Word of God and the sacraments (baptism and Holy Communion for Lutherans) were God's gifts by which his special blessing and grace come to us.

Not all Lutherans would agree, but perhaps this is what "full gospel" (Pentecostal/charismatic) people mean by "the anointing" and what the ancient Hebrews called the *Shechinah*, the manifestation of God's *special* presence (in contrast to his *general* presence, or omnipresence). That is to say, Christians everywhere have believed that God shows up in special ways under special circumstances, which is my loose definition of "sacrament": *transformational encounter with God.*

The Catholics' sacrament of confession refers to every believer's obligation not only to confess sins to God, but also to share them with a priest in confessional privacy. This *can* become a religious avoidance behavior, a forgiveness catchall for a person with little or no intention of changing. However, *most Protestants*—many of whom scorn the need for priests who in some way mediate between the people and God—*confess nothing*.

This is what I've said to my congregation: Most of you haven't confessed a single sin to anyone anytime in the last five years. In fact, it probably hasn't even entered your mind that doing so is helpful in any way, even though the Bible clearly tells us, "Confess your sins to each other and pray for each other so that you may be healed." Why? Because "the prayer of a righteous man is powerful and effective."[16] Confession is about my getting things right with God, but remarkably the apostle James is teaching us here that wholeness in my life is probably not possible outside of my deep relationship with others in the community of faith.

I've discovered this personally, and I wrote about it extensively in *Leaders That Last*, coauthored with Alfred Ells.[17] I have no doubt that my own spiritual and emotional health depends on my relationships with significant people in my life. Accordingly, confession of sin is both a personal spiritual practice and a shared activity of the faith community. It's not good for man to be alone.[18] I need others to love and accept me in spite of the way I am, to forgive me, and to hold me accountable. *I need others as much as I need God.*

As I see it, this might very well be the most neglected element of Protestant faith and worship. Our Protestant *and* American heritage is so fiercely independent that we've largely lost the biblical model of community, where we share *everything* in common—joy and sorrow, gain and loss, righteousness and sin. My success is your success. My failure is your failure. We're in this together. Forever.

So if you really want to be free from the slavery of an addiction, or a dysfunction, or a propensity toward failure, or sin in any aspect of your life (that would be all of us, every one of us), consider these elements of commitment to a twelve-step program:

- The problem starts with you, and you, personally, are powerless in the face of your problem.

- You need a Higher Power.

- You need a group and regular times with that group, and the group needs to be both safe and honest.

- You need a "sponsor," a mentoring relationship with someone you trust.

Confession is a sacrament because the community of faith is sacramental. This is where God's special presence visits us and attends our souls, as Jesus promised: "Where two or three come together in my name, *there am I with them.*"[19]

Confession is also a simple way to take up your cross and die to yourself. There are few things more painful than telling someone else about your failure. Ironically, though, there are few things more transformational than telling someone else about your failure and asking them to pray for you.

Viewpoint #3:
The Cross is an exit door from the power of habitual sin.

SCRIPTURE

†3M "Grace and peace to you from God our Father and the Lord Jesus Christ, who gave himself for our sins to rescue us from the present evil age, according to the will of our God and Father."[20]

†3Tu "Through Christ Jesus the law of the Spirit of life set me free from the law of sin and death. For what the law [that is, human effort] was powerless to do in that it was weakened by the sinful nature, God did by sending his own Son in the likeness of sinful man to be a sin offering. And so he condemned sin in sinful man, in order that the righteous requirements of the law might be fully met in us, who do not live according to the sinful nature but according to the Spirit."[21]

†3W "Those controlled by the sinful nature cannot please God. You, however, are controlled not by the sinful nature but by the Spirit, if the Spirit of God lives in you. And if anyone does not have the Spirit of Christ, he does not belong to Christ. But if Christ is in you, your body is dead because of sin, yet your spirit is alive because of righteousness."[22]

†3Th "We know that our old self was crucified with him so that the body of sin might be done away with, that we should no longer be slaves to sin—because anyone who has died has been freed from sin.

"Now if we died with Christ, we believe that we will also live with him. For we know that since Christ was raised from the dead, he cannot die again; death no longer has mastery over him. The death he died, he died to sin once for all; but the life he lives, he lives to God.

"In the same way, count yourselves dead to sin but alive to God in Christ Jesus."[23]

†3F "'I am thirsty.'"[24]

†3Sa "Do not let sin reign in your mortal body so that you obey its evil desires. Do not offer the parts of your body to sin, as instruments of wickedness, but rather offer yourselves to God, as those who have been brought from death to life; and offer the parts of your body to him as instruments of righteousness. For sin shall not be your master, because you are not under law, but under grace."[25]

†3Su "Don't you know that when you offer yourselves to someone to obey him as slaves, you are slaves to the one whom you obey—whether you are slaves to sin, which leads to death, or to obedience, which leads to righteousness? But thanks be to God that, though you used to be slaves to sin, you whole-heartedly obeyed the form of teaching to which you were entrusted."[26]

CHAPTER EIGHT

Yes, Virginia, There Is a Devil

Viewpoint #4:
The Cross is an exit door from the power of evil.

"Lead us not into temptation."
—Jesus

Evil is real, and there is an evil empire.

Daily I have difficulty with my old self, my sinful nature, that was crucified with Christ, but I must face the fact that the smoldering embers of my dark side are fanned by the hot winds of the under-world. In *The Matrix,* people not only are bound by a captivating illusion, the virtual reality of a computer-generated world, but that "reality" is also sustained by the power of AI, artificial intelligence. I'd like to suggest that our own world is empowered by AI, *alternative* intelligence.

In my book *Winning Your Spiritual Battles*,[1] an exploration of spiritual conflict, I explain that the dark side of the spiritual realm can hold us captive, that there are several "strongholds"[2] of resistance to God and his kingdom. Let's consider two of these.

First, there are what I call *personal strongholds:* weaknesses, habits, dysfunctions, addictions.[3] Each of these can be addressed through confession, prayer, counsel, and therapy, but according to the New Testament, our weaknesses often interface with the dark side of the spiritual dimension. For example, Paul writes, "In your anger do not sin. . . . *Do not give the devil a foothold.*"[4] Is this true? Is this reality—that the devil can enter your life when you get angry? That anger is potentially a phone booth in hell?

Certainly this is not an idea welcomed in the Western world, at least not in the contemporary West, the "enlightened" culture in which naturalism has essentially robbed us of our sense of the mystical, the transcendent, the divine. Just a few weeks ago I heard a radio talk-show host speaking about "supernatural" elements in Mel Gibson's *The Passion of the Christ.* He said something like this: "People in those days were more likely to relate sudden events in nature, like lightning and thunder, to a specific act of God."

Um . . . people "in those days"?

In *one* sense I agree: Our world has come a long way, in that societies immersed in superstition and obsessed with witchcraft don't make good places to live. Well-informed media voices, though, don't seem to know that *most* of the world *still* thinks there is a direct link between the spiritual and natural realms.[5] Only in the West have we come to believe that everything can be rationally explained, that there *never* is a direct link between (for instance) a storm and God, or an illness and the devil.

A NEW AGE

Science has taken us throughout the galaxy and hopefully will help us find cures for cancer and AIDS. The world in the new millennium, though, is experiencing an unanticipated resurgence of spirituality and fascination with the supernatural. Harvey Cox, Distinguished

Professor of Divinity at Harvard University, who in his late sixties wrote controversially about the secular city and the death of God, has in the last few years become a student of the extraordinary worldwide revival of religion. In his bestselling *Fire From Heaven: The Rise of Pentecostal Spirituality and the Reshaping of Religion in the 21st Century,*[6] Cox admits that with what just a few decades ago appeared to be a declining interest in spirituality, he never could have predicted such an epoch-making revival of global religion.

As for me, I believe. I believe in God. I believe that Jesus Christ is his Son. That Jesus died on the cross for our sins. That evil is real, and that our thoughts and behaviors interface with both the light and dark elements of the spiritual realm: "He who does what is sinful is of the devil, because the devil has been sinning from the beginning. The reason the Son of God appeared was to destroy the devil's work."[7]

DEMONIC INFLUENCE

Not every wicked thought, not every bad behavior, is the direct result of demonic influence, but many thoughts and behaviors are, and if I live my life as if evil isn't real, then evil couldn't be happier. Last week someone in my church told me that the terrorist who flew the plane into the Pentagon on 9/11 was her business client. As you might expect, she was interviewed by FBI agents. "He was as pleasant as he could be—a good customer," she told them. One of them replied, "I guess he was doing his job well, then, wasn't he?"

Just today as I was driving, I listened to National Public Radio reports on how, before 9/11, *both* the Clinton and Bush administrations downplayed, even ignored threats from Osama bin Laden and al-Queda. Regardless of whether these reports were entirely accurate, this is like the devil's plan exactly: The less you know about his secret world and the less you believe in the reality of evil, the more potential power he wields in your life.

The apostle Peter cautioned Christ-followers to "be self-controlled and alert. Your enemy the devil prowls around like a roaring lion looking for someone to devour. *Resist him, standing firm in the faith.*"[8]

And how do we do that?

- By acknowledging the reality of evil

- By living in God's light, by taking his Word seriously, because we know that darkness in our lives is a phone booth in hell, an entry point for the devil, out of his world and into ours

- By confessing our sins to God and to one another

- By standing daily in the shadow of the Cross, where Christ cast down the devil and his hosts[9]

Second, there are what I call *ideological strongholds:* commonly held ideas and beliefs that may have intrinsic spiritual power. Consider this extraordinary passage:

> They [the people of Jesus' hometown] took offense at him. But Jesus said to them, "Only in his hometown and in his own house is a prophet without honor." *And he did not do many miracles there because of their lack of faith.*
> MATTHEW 13:57–58, EMPHASIS MINE

This particular community was bound by a pervasive spirit of unbelief that hindered the healing power of the Son of God himself. I heard an echo of this recently when a prominent Chinese church leader, speaking to an American audience, observed, "I can see why it is so difficult to be a Christian in your country. *You have so many distractions.*"

RED OCTOBER

Some years ago, just after the fall of communism, I led a ministry team to Krasnodar, a large Russian city near the Black Sea, to present public lectures on New Age religion and spiritual warfare. Accompanying me was my friend, scholar and author Doug Groothuis. Between sessions, he and I, both keen on history, visited a local museum.

One of the museum's rooms was dedicated entirely to the 1917 Revolution, "Red October." When we stepped into that space, the brilliantly red flags and banners took our breath away. As we stood there in stilled awe of an era that warped world history, Doug said to me in hushed tones, "Little could Karl Marx have imagined the impact of his life as he sat alone at his candlelit desk writing the *Communist Manifesto*. This room is a metaphor of the power of ideas."

> They crucified him with the criminals. Which is more amazing, to find Jesus in such bad company or to find the criminals in such good company? . . .
>
> Jesus died precisely for these two criminals who were crucified on his right and left and went to their death with him. He did not die for the sake of a good world, he died for the sake of an evil world.
>
> —Karl Barth

Ideas create our perceptions of reality, and the kingdom of darkness is often the engine of these ideas. Among the worst ideologies is racism: commonly shared, unquestioned ideas about "those people," which can be anyone other than "us." The holocaust and other "ethnic cleansings" are screaming examples of the perverse consequences of mass ideological delusion. Today our world is in the vise of, on the one hand, Western military power and its "Christian" culture, and, on the other hand, ageless, relentless, merciless Muslim extremism. These battles have been raging for hundreds of years. President Bush and others are going to "stamp out evil"? I don't think so.

I do commend the efforts of global leaders to make our world a safer place, and I'm personally involved in reconciliation efforts in the Middle East. Governments can somewhat control evil,[10] but they can't eliminate it. Evil has deeper roots than an ideological gulf between the bourgeoisie and the proletariat, or between Palestinians and Israelis. There will not be true peace on earth without God's direct intervention.

Yes, the Bible tells us to pray for the peace of Jerusalem,[11] and I do, nearly every day. But the Bible also says the world as we know it will end not far from the Holy City, in the Valley of Megiddo, where the globe's massed armies will self-destruct in the Battle of Armageddon. When in the end man destroys himself and his world, he won't do it alone. Hell will be his ally.

This is precisely the view of John's Revelation, the very last and most mysterious of the Bible's sixty-six books. John describes the end of human history in terms of outright evil. Here are some of the key events that show clearly the intercourse (inter-curse?) between the dominion of darkness and the kingdoms, systems, and values of "the world."

Elements of world government and particular leaders, including the Antichrist (aka "the beast"), are in direct alliance with Satan.

> The whole world was astonished and followed the beast. Men worshiped the dragon [Satan] because he had given authority to the beast. . . . He opened his mouth to blaspheme God, and to slander his name and his dwelling place and those who live in heaven. He was given power to make war against the saints and to conquer them. And he was given authority over every tribe, people, language and nation.[12]

World empires and many of their systems are unwittingly allied against God and his righteous purposes, and as a consequence invite his wrath. Ironically, while Karl Marx was proposing that "religion is the opiate of the people," he was in fact offering his own drug for the masses. Countless millions of innocent people died as a direct result of his ideology.[13]

World economies, at their core, are godless and self-serving. A case can be made that their enmeshment with godless world governments is in alliance with hell. Jesus said we "can't serve two masters . . . both God and Money,"[14] and the term he used for money, *Mammon,* was widely considered a name for a dark spiritual entity, an actual demon.

I have no doubt spiritual forces are at work in many of materialism's ideological underpinnings. Often we're possessed by our possessions. Consumer debt? If it isn't a demon, it controls people, even destroys lives and families in a manner worthy of hell itself. Money isn't inherently bad, but the *love* of money is the root of all kinds of evil.[15]

Armageddon is not merely a clash of godless nations but also an alliance of witless national leaders against God and his people.

> Why do the nations conspire and the peoples plot in vain? The kings of the earth take their stand and the rulers gather together against the LORD and against his Anointed One. "Let us

break their chains," they say, "and throw off their fetters." The One enthroned in heaven laughs; the Lord scoffs at them.[16]

IT'S A SPIRITUAL PROBLEM

According to the Bible, then, every problem is ultimately and fundamentally spiritual. You didn't hear me say that every problem is *exclusively* spiritual. Human life is a convergence of time and space, now and forever, material and immaterial, but every problem—and every solution to every problem—is *essentially* spiritual. Paul presents it this way:

> It is true that I am an ordinary, weak human being, but I don't use human plans and methods to win my battles. I use God's mighty weapons, not those made by men, to knock down the devil's strongholds.
>
> 2 CORINTHIANS 10:3–4 TLB

"The fear of the Lord is the beginning of knowledge," wrote Solomon. "In all your ways acknowledge him, and he will make your paths straight."[17] Either God will be the starting line of your blessed life, or his judgment will be your bitter end.

The world is inhabited by sinful humanity empowered by the evil side of the universe, but Christ is coming back to right the wrong world, to establish his rule and dominion forever. Like God, Satan has an "only son," the Antichrist, whose goal is to rule with an iron fist over a godless world of the devil's making. Nevertheless, the ancient prophet Isaiah foretells that Christ will strike down the Antichrist with a rod of iron:

> To us a child is born, to us a son is given, and the government will be on his shoulders. And he will be called Wonderful Counselor, Mighty God, Everlasting Father, Prince of Peace.

Most of us have heard choirs sing this at Christmas, but there's more:

> *Of the increase of his government and peace there will be no end.* He will reign on David's throne and over his kingdom, establish-

ing and upholding it with justice and righteousness from that time on and forever. The zeal of the LORD Almighty will accomplish this.[18]

Again: "*Of the increase of his government and peace there will be no end.*"

Wherever Messiah is King, wherever God is in control—in my home or in my homeland—there's peace. And note the correlation between government and peace. More of God's government, more peace. I have to believe—and I've seen it time and time again—that peace becomes more elusive the less people submit to the government of God. Listen:

> I tell you this, and insist on it in the Lord, that you must no longer live as the Gentiles do, in the futility of their thinking. They are darkened in their understanding and separated from the life of God because of the ignorance that is in them due to the hardening of their hearts.
>
> EPHESIANS 4:17–18

Personal and ideological strongholds are as real as . . . well . . . the Matrix. So like Neo, relentlessly searching for the truth, we need to think twice about everything we think. Question everything we believe about this life. If we want mental wholeness and spiritual freedom, every idea needs to be examined in the bright light of God's Word, and every thought must be submitted to the law of Christ.[19]

Yes, Virginia, there *is* a devil. Thank God for the Cross, a holy place where we are delivered from the power of sin and death and reconciled to God and to one another. It takes more than a village: It takes a miracle. The Cross of Christ is our only hope, our only exit door from the dark theater of horror.

Look what the Bible has to say about the Cross of Christ and its power over spiritual darkness. . . .

Viewpoint #4:
The Cross is an exit door from the power of evil.

SCRIPTURE

†4M "He has rescued us from the dominion of darkness and
brought us into the kingdom of the Son he loves, in whom

we have redemption, the forgiveness of sins."[20]

†4Tu "Having canceled the written code, with its regulations, that was against us and that stood opposed to us, he took it away, nailing it to the cross. And having disarmed the powers and authorities, he made a public spectacle of them, triumphing over them by the cross."[21]

†4W "He who does what is sinful is of the devil, because the devil has been sinning from the beginning. The reason the Son of God appeared was to destroy the devil's work."[22]

†4Th "'I [Jesus] am sending you to them to open their eyes and turn them from darkness to light, and from the power of Satan to God, so that they may receive forgiveness of sins and a place among those who are sanctified by faith in me.'"[23]

†4F "'Father, into your hands I commit my spirit.'"[24]

†4Sa "Even if our gospel is veiled, it is veiled to those who are per-ishing. The god of this age has blinded the minds of unbeliev-ers, so that they cannot see the light of the gospel of the glory of Christ, who is the image of God."[25]

†4Su "God anointed Jesus of Nazareth with the Holy Spirit and power, and . . . he went around doing good and healing all who were under the power of the devil, because God was with him."[26]

CHAPTER NINE

Going Nowhere Fast

Viewpoint #5:
*The perfect, finished work of Christ on the cross is an exit door
from the treadmill of religious effort.*

If the bad outweighs the good, you go to hell; if the good outweighs the bad, you go to heaven.
—Muhammad Ali

Through the law [human effort] I died to the law [human effort]
so that I might live for God. I have been crucified with Christ and
I no longer live, but Christ lives in me.
—Paul

God helps those who help themselves.

What in the world does that mean? The "pretty good person"
(who thinks this statement is in the Bible) believes it means that God
smiles on those who try hardest or at least do a little bit "better" than

others. He or she might say something like this:

> Compared to other people, I'm a pretty good person. When I think about my life, I have to admit I've done some not-so-great things, but my life isn't nearly as bad as the lives of others I know. If God is paying attention, he'll probably agree. And if I *have* done something really wrong, well, the God I believe in will overlook it.

So who's going to hell? Nobody, really. Except maybe Hitler. Yeah, Hitler's in hell. And Saruman, the evil wizard from *Lord of the Rings*. And Orcs, those slimy slaves in need of serious dental work.

And then there are rapists and serial killers on death row. But are they actually bad people? Or are they pretty good people most of the time? Someone I know who works in a federal penitentiary told me that he has yet to meet an inmate who felt like he was supposed to be there, that he deserved to be there. Every felon thinks that, basically, except for a crime or two, he's not really a bad person.

You may have heard about the longest hostage crisis in U.S. prison history, right here in Arizona. Two prisoners, already serving multiple life sentences, were able to break into a guard tower, and the authorities stood helpless as the men held a female guard hostage for weeks. After the inmates finally surrendered, a local radio station was able to finagle an interview with one of them, and not once in an extended conversation did the man suggest that in any way was he responsible for the ordeal. No, from the perspective of his warped reality, what happened was a failure of the prison system. Admittedly, certain things need to change in our correctional institutions. Contrary to popular opinion, prisons are *not* resorts. But surely our justice system doesn't consistently incarcerate the wrong people.

Even someone who acknowledges being a bad person will probably tell you it's because of the circumstances of his difficult and painful life. He'd be quick to tell you that if you walked down the same dark alley of life, you'd likely be in jail too. And there's truth in that, you know—who are we to judge?

So who's pretty good and who's pretty bad? The implication here is that God grades on a curve, but where do we draw the line? Where does *God* draw the line? Is there a point between perfect and perverted when God says your life is okay? That you get at least a passing grade? How high do you have to score?

80%?

65%?

Top half?

Do you know? Does any religion or denomination know?

Religious scorekeeping is on a curve, but think about it: *Everything* about your life as you know it is on a curve. We live in a universe of comparisons. In a sick sort of way, when I realize that I'm better than somebody else—and I only have to be *slightly* better (just ask a bobsled team)—it makes me feel better about myself (at least, *sort of* better).

> As long as I keep running about, asking: "Do you love me? Do you really love me?" I give all power to the voices of the world and put myself in bondage because the world is filled with "ifs." The world says: "Yes, I love you *if* you are good-looking, intelligent, and wealthy. I love you *if* you have a good education, a good job, and good connections. I love you *if* you produce much, sell much, and buy much." There are endless "ifs" hidden in the world's love. The "ifs" enslave me, since it is impossible to respond adequately to all of them. The world's love will always be conditional.
>
> —Henri Nouwen, *The Return of the Prodigal Son*

MEGA-MEANINGLESS

I'm the pastor of a *mega*-church, one of the largest in North America. Yet when I visit the massive Willow Creek Church campus, I don't know whether to laugh or cry, to praise God or feel depressed. One of my best friends from college wrote me recently, "I must admit I feel somewhat intimidated by the things you have accomplished: writing books, pastoring a mega-church, raising famous children. I know what the Lord requires of me is faithfulness with what he has entrusted to me, but it is still difficult when I see my peers having greater recognition than I do."

It's all relative.

Just tonight I was having an evening meal with a group of Christian leaders, all of them fine men of God. As we shared around the table, one of them surprised us when he brought us back to our conversation at lunch. "Earlier today," he said softly, "several of you were talking about all your education." (I was one of them.) "Well," he continued somewhat defiantly, "I never finished high school, and God is still using me."

How about these comparisons:

- How tall are you?

- Are you beautiful or ugly?

- Do you have a radio voice or a squeaky voice?

- How's your hair? Do you have hair?

- Where do you work? What kind of job do you have?

- Are you a supervisor or a subordinate?

- How much money do you make?

- What kind of car do you drive? A Mercedes? Wow! A twelve-year-old Mercedes. Oh.

- Do you have a house or an apartment? How many bedrooms? How many square feet? New furniture, or cheap old stuff from a garage sale?

- How are your kids doing? Lettering in sports? Getting straight A's? Failing?

- And one of the most devastating comparisons of all: What color is your skin?

It's all relative.

CURVES AHEAD

The curve is a curse. Deep inside we hate comparisons, but we're obsessed with better-than, smarter-than, richer-than, bigger-than, faster-than, more points than. Stupidly, we roll this curse of the curve into our religion and entertain thoughts like *I'm more spiritual* or *I'm a relatively good person,* as if God thinks this way too. As if he compares us to others.

When people believe that "God helps those who help themselves," they must also believe, conversely, that God doesn't help those who don't help themselves. Very simply, if you're good, if you're livin' right, God will love you and bless you. If you're not, you might be on your way to hell.

In a recent issue of *Reader's Digest,* the editor asked Muhammad Ali to talk about his faith, to which he replied,

> [It] means a ticket to heaven. One day we're all going to die, and God's going to judge us, [our] good and bad deeds. [If the] bad outweighs the good, you go to hell; if the good outweighs the bad, you go to heaven.[1]

This, by the way, is the central idea of Darwinian theory, that life is the survival of the fittest. Yes, evolution grades everybody on the curve and shows no mercy. So does every religion on planet earth, *except the Christian faith.* Christianity is the *only* religion where relationship with God is based entirely on *grace:* God's utterly unconditional love, acceptance, and forgiveness.

The curve is a huge problem, because the less grace in your God, the less grace you have for yourself. In addition, the more you feel you have to work on achieving your own salvation, the less grace you have for other people. This is why some religious people can be so nasty and intolerant: they think God is that way. He grades them on his curve, they grade others on theirs. This, of course, only compounds the problem, because if you do "score high" on the religious curve, you increase the likelihood someone who really knows you will call you a hypocrite. When your life is on the curve, you just can't win. If you win the rat race, you're still a rat!

A PERFECT "10"

Let's go back to those percentages. If God really does grade us on the curve, then where do we fall off the curve into hell? At what point does God say, "I can't take this anymore! I can't stand *you* anymore! I'm not going to help you, because you're not helping yourself as much as I think you should." Here's exactly where God draws the line: *You have to have a* perfect *score.* Not 99.99 percent. *100 percent.* No exceptions.

Okay, I'll admit it. Just about everyone is a pretty good person, but this is just as true: *Everyone* from time to time is a pretty *bad* person. Like criminals in the federal penitentiary . . . and you and me. Yet on God's religion-and-good-works test, we can't score a nano-fraction less than 100 percent. We have to do all the right things for all the right reasons at all the right times, as James wrote: "Whoever keeps the whole law and yet stumbles at just one point is guilty of breaking all of it."[2]

So you've kept the law? You've obeyed the Ten Commandments? Well, don't forget what Jesus said, that if in a fit of rage you call somebody a jerk, you've broken the sixth commandment and are close to hell.[3] Or if you look at the opposite sex lustfully, you've broken the seventh commandment and are guilty of adultery.[4] In fact, "unless your righteousness surpasses that of the Pharisees and the teachers of the law, you will certainly not enter the kingdom of heaven."[5]

Curses! Because it's at this point you realize the curve is a curse. It's like running the Boston Marathon against some guy from Kenya. You know he's going to win. You know you don't have a chance, but for whatever irrational reason, you tell yourself, "Maybe, just maybe, I can win this thing." And race after race the Kenyan finishes hours ahead of you.

DEMOTIVATORS

Have you seen despair.com? Founder E. L. Kersten had a brilliant idea: design and market "demotivational" posters. You know, like those big, black-bordered, framed pictures you see hanging around offices and airports? Where under a fantastic photo is a word like "courage," or "perseverance," along with an inspirational thought? Well, despair.com inverts the concept, promising, "No matter who you are, you have the potential to be so very much less. And with the transformative powers of our Demotivators® products, you will be." One of the despair.com posters reminds me of religion. It shows an exhausted runner sitting on a bench and hanging his head; it almost seems he's looking right at the caption:

LOSING:
When your very best isn't good enough.

That would be a "pretty good" runner.

So how are you doing on your New Year's resolutions? How's your righteousness lately? Pretty good, but never quite good enough? Is your very best not good enough for God?

You might come back at me, "Maybe not good enough for *your* God, but good enough for *mine.*" Okay, then, so you've mellowed out your God a little? You can't quite live up to God, so you get God to live down to you?

• **Objection: But it's impossible to score 100 percent in God's test of life!** *Right!* We can't even live up to our own expectations for ourselves, let alone God's! This is why Jesus told Nicodemus, a very good and religious man, "You must be born again."[6] In other words, you can be as good as you can be, and it won't be enough. Salvation through human effort always falls short, because from God's point of view we don't have a *behavior* problem, we have a *nature* problem.

God isn't just hoping for us to be a little better than we are or as good as we can be. If I understand Jesus correctly, when he tells Nicodemus he must be born again, he is effectively telling him that he needs a new nature. Moral improvement isn't enough. Something is wrong in the core of his being.

Looking Nicodemus straight in the eye, his own eyes bright with the light of God on that dark night, Jesus said (I paraphrase), "You're as good as you'll ever be, but that won't bleach your tainted soul. Instead, you need a new soul, a new nature. Right now you have the DNA of death. You need the DNA of life—you need to be born anew. You need to be regenerated: re-*gene*-erated!"

What's impossible, humanly speaking, is possible with God. Grace is not God's good help for those who are deserving, it's his radical intervention in the lives of those who *cannot* help themselves.

• **Objection: If God expects 100 percent, then God is way too demanding. I can't serve that kind of God.** It's not that God is demanding: it's that God is perfect. Fortunately, he has taken the initiative to solve the problem. *Religion* says, "There's a problem between me and God, and I have to do something about it." *God* says, "There is a problem between me and people. I have to do something about it." And he did: "God so loved the world that he gave his one and only Son, that whoever believes in him shall not perish but have eternal life."[7]

Religious people have tried and tried, and failed and failed, and finally found the grace of God, like Paul:

> You know my pedigree: a legitimate birth, circumcised on the eighth day; an Israelite from the elite tribe of Benjamin; a strict and devout adherent to God's law; a fiery defender of the purity of my religion, even to the point of persecuting Christians; a meticulous observer of everything set down in God's law Book.
>
> The very credentials these people are waving around as something special, I'm tearing up and throwing out with the trash—along with everything else I used to take credit for. And why? Because of Christ. Yes, all the things I once thought were so important are gone from my life.
>
> Compared to the high privilege of knowing Christ Jesus as my Master, firsthand, everything I once thought I had going for me is insignificant—dog dung. I've dumped it all in the trash so that I could embrace Christ and be embraced by him. I didn't want some petty, inferior brand of righteousness that comes from keeping a list of rules when I could get the robust kind that comes from trusting Christ—God's righteousness. I gave up all that inferior stuff so I could know Christ personally, experience his resurrection power, be a partner in his suffering, and go all the way with him to death itself.
>
> PHILIPPIANS 3:4–10 THE MESSAGE

BETTER THAN YOU

Let me talk about myself for a minute. Impress you with some of my credentials. I'm a pastor. Same wife for thirty-three years. No sex before our honeymoon. Kids and grandkids love God. Two seminary degrees. I've talked to thousands of people about God and the Bible. And helped them. I go to church three times a week.

Wouldn't you agree? I'm way up there on the curve. Hey, if you're reading this book and haven't been to church in years . . . you think *you're* a pretty good person? I just hope God loves you as much as he loves me.

Getting sick yet? You see, the more people brag about their success, about themselves, the more it makes you want to puke. And the very worst is when people are proud of their religion: it neutralizes whatever good they've actually done. The downside of working really hard to be good is knowing you're good, and that makes people around you ill.

Here's what sounds like a demotivator from the Bible: "All of us have become like one who is unclean, and all our *righteous acts* are like filthy rags; we all shrivel up like a leaf, and like the wind our sins sweep us away."[8] Do you see that? It's not our *unrighteous acts* that are like filthy rags, it's our *righteousness*! Why would that be?

Let's make another visit to the doctor's office. How would your physician feel if, when he diagnosed a serious illness in your body, you told him, "It's okay, Doc. I'm fine. I know you just told me I'm dying, but I can take care of this. I'm up to the challenge."

He would tell you, "There's nothing I can do to help you if you refuse to believe there's something wrong." This is why terribly religious people have a terribly hard time loving God. They've come to believe so much in themselves. Jesus said to a Pharisee about a prostitute: "I tell you, her many sins have been forgiven—for she loved much. But he who has been forgiven little loves little."[9]

This statement about "filthy rags" in Isaiah is not actually a demotivator. It's a diagnosis of the human condition in the hope that we'll accept necessary and radical treatment. This note from the wife of a good friend of mine just popped up in my email *today:*

We are writing to update you and ask for your prayers for my husband as he faces treatment for a type of B cell lymphoma called Waldenstrom's Macroglobulinemia, a very rare form of cancer of the lymph system. Though it has been diagnosed as indolent, or slow growing, the disease has progressed to the point where the diseased B cells are crowding out the production of normal red and white cells and platelets in the bone marrow, so the oncologist has recommended treatment immediately.

I know this man well. He's a fine guy. A godly man. As a pastor, I've had to walk with people through these kinds of things way too many times. Right now I'm sitting here clenching my teeth, wagging my head in denial. "No, no," I'm telling myself. "Not again. Not *another* friend with cancer."

> All men indeed desire good, and pretend to something good in what they say and do; therefore, under the appearance of good, many are deceived.
> —Thomas à Kempis

THE BLOODY TRUTH

Cancer is nasty. So are "filthy rags," which in the Hebrew text of the Old Testament literally means "menstrual cloths." As a woman said to me just a couple of weeks ago, this refers to the blood of death, in contrast to the blood of life in the sacrifice of Christ. When a woman bleeds during her time of the month, her body is telling her she's *not* pregnant. There's no new life there.

Yes, it's a vulgar but poignant word picture of our "righteousness": lifeless, even repulsive to God. Something to be disdained. *Why* is our righteousness so "filthy"? Because it's a dirty trick. It fools us into thinking we don't really need the righteousness of God in Christ. Our own rightness is like Antichrist in our hearts. Not that we are blatantly against Jesus, because that's not what *anti-christ* actually means. In Greek, *anti* means, more precisely, "instead of." Antichrist is not just anti-Christ: He's a devious substitute. *Like our own righteousness.*

This is why Paul summed up in one word all the good in his best life as a very religious man: *rubbish.*

As for legalistic righteousness, [I was] faultless. But whatever

[I thought] was to my profit I now consider loss for the sake of Christ. . . . I consider them rubbish, *that I may gain Christ and be found in him, not having a righteousness of my own.*

PHILIPPIANS 3:6–9

Rubbish is another crude word, meaning, literally, "dog droppings."

Ironically, the harder we try to be good, the more our religious effort isolates us from the very love and grace of God we imagine we can earn:

- You who are trying to be justified by law have been alienated from Christ; you have fallen away from grace.[10]

- Christ is useless to you if you are counting on clearing your debt to God by keeping those laws; you are lost from God's grace.[11]

- I suspect you would never intend this, but this is what happens. When you attempt to live by your own religious plans and projects, you are cut off from Christ, you fall out of grace.[12]

Earlier I bragged about myself, but the truth of the matter is that I feel just like Paul did: I am what I am because of the grace of God. All the religious success in my life doesn't give me an ounce of confidence that I'm going to heaven. My only hope—and yours—is to trust in what Jesus did on the cross.

The alternative to Christ's perfect, finished work is religion, human effort, what the New Testament (especially Paul) calls "the law." For Paul, it's either one or the other. Law or grace. Limited human effort or the limitless power of God. People helping themselves helplessly or God coming to the rescue of the helpless.

The bloody truth is that when Christ died on the cross, he did it to save you from your *unrighteousness,* but he also came to set you free from the limitations and inadequacy of your own *righteousness.*

Viewpoint #5:
The perfect, finished work of Christ on the cross is an exit door from the treadmill of religious effort.

SCRIPTURE

†5M   "There is now no condemnation for those who are in Christ Jesus, because through Christ Jesus the law of the Spirit of life [God's effort] set me free from the law of sin and death [human effort]. For what the law [human effort] was powerless to do in that it was weakened by the sinful nature, God did by sending his own Son in the likeness of sinful man to be a sin offering. And so he condemned sin in sinful man, in order that the righteous requirements of the law [God's expectations] might be fully met in us, who do not live according to the sinful nature but according to the Spirit."[13]

†5Tu   "Since they [Israel] did not know the righteousness that comes from God and sought to establish their own, they did not submit to God's righteousness. Christ is the end of the law [human effort] so that there may be righteousness for everyone who believes.
"Moses describes in this way the righteousness that is by the law [human effort]: 'The man who does these things will live by them.'"[14]

†5W   "Let no debt remain outstanding, except the continuing debt to love one another, for he who loves his fellowman has fulfilled the law [God's expectations]. The commandments, 'Do not commit adultery,' 'Do not murder,' 'Do not steal,' 'Do not covet,' and whatever other commandment there may be, are summed up in this one rule: 'Love your neighbor as yourself.' Love does no harm to its neighbor. Therefore love is the fulfillment of the law [God's expectations]."[15]

†5Th   "The sting of death is sin, and the power of sin is the law [the limits of human effort to please God]. But thanks be to

God! He gives us the victory through our Lord Jesus Christ."[16]

†5F "He said to his mother, 'Dear woman, here is your son,' and to [John] the disciple, 'Here is your mother.'"[17]

†5Sa "All who rely on observing the law [human effort] are under a curse, for it is written: 'Cursed is everyone who does not continue to do everything written in the Book of the Law.' Clearly no one is justified before God by the law, because 'The righteous will live by faith.' The law [getting into relationship with God] is not based on faith; on the contrary, 'The man who does these things will live by them.' Christ redeemed us from the curse of the law [the curse of the curve of human effort] by becoming a curse for us, for it is written: 'Cursed is everyone who is hung on a tree.' He redeemed us in order that the blessing given to Abraham might come to the Gentiles through Christ Jesus, so that by faith we might receive the promise of the Spirit."[18]
"Know that a man is not justified by observing the law [human effort], but by faith in Jesus Christ. So we, too, have put our faith in Christ Jesus that we may be justified by faith in Christ and not by observing the law [well-intentioned human effort], because by observing the law no one will be justified."[19]

†5Su "Through the law [human effort] I died to the law [human effort] so that I might live for God. I have been crucified with Christ and I no longer live, but Christ lives in me. The life I live in the body, I live by faith in the Son of God, who loved me and gave himself for me. I do not set aside the grace of God, for if righteousness could be gained through the law [human effort], Christ died for nothing!"[20]

CHAPTER TEN

Extreme Life

Viewpoint #6:
The Cross is the portal to extreme life.

Welcome to the Desert of the Real.
    —Morpheus

As for you, you were dead in your transgressions and sins, in
which you used to live when you followed the ways of this world
and of the ruler of the kingdom of the air, the spirit who is now
at work in those who are disobedient.
    —Ephesians 2:1–2

Christ-life is extreme.

The Cross isn't just about what God gets you out of, an exit from
sin, shame, and religious legalism. *The Cross of Christ is also about what
God gets you into, and what God gets into you.* The Cross is a portal, an
entry point into what Jesus called "abundant life": "I am come that

they might have life, and that they might have it more *abundantly*."¹

The Greek word here is extreme, meaning "extraordinary, remarkable, that which is not usually encountered among men, going beyond what is necessary."² Jesus could not have used a more deeply significant term—maybe today he would call it "extreme life."

Everybody wants to be extreme, as in extreme reality television. Extreme candid camera: *Jackass,* at times extremely funny, most times extremely disgusting. Extreme sports: *X-Games.* Extreme sex: alcohol and Viagra. And now there's extreme Gatorade, which makes me gag.

But are these things *real* life? Or just a rush? Is living on the edge *really* living? Or is life just an orgasm, and then you die? Last night I noticed what looked like two giant mosquitoes mating on the wall of my bedroom. An hour or so later, they were still there. I interrupted them. This morning, one of them was near death, quivering on the cold bathroom counter. I guess it was sex to die for.

People want life beyond limits—life outside the lines—*every one of us wants our life to mean something.* Every one of us ultimately wants real life, not just a buzz. When Jesus offers us extreme life, though, it's not about what happens *to* us, it's what happens *in* us. Extreme life isn't out there somewhere, at the top of the highest mountain, or down the most incredible Black Diamond ski slope. Extreme life is not what you do but who you are. Instead of "What is truth?" today Pilate might ask, "What is life?" or "What's the meaning of life?"

EXTREME LIFE

Extreme life is what the Bible refers to as "life that is truly life."³ It's eternal life, but not only life that goes on forever: It's *life in this life that's infused with God's very life.* It's life we encounter and experience in the crucifixion and resurrection of Christ:

> "I am the resurrection and the *life*. He who believes in me
> will *live,* even though he dies; and whoever *lives* and believes
> in me [*into* me] will never die. Do you believe this?"
>
> JOHN 11:25–26, EMPHASIS MINE

Zôê, the Greek term for "life," used in this text (see italics above), means "the supernatural life belonging to God and Christ, which believers will receive in the future, but which they also enjoy here and now. . . . [It's] life for those who have come out of the state of death."[4] In contrast to the Greek word *bios,* which is used to refer to the more basic, physical elements of life, *zôé* is Christ-life, Spirit-life to the extreme.

Here's how I define *zôé* in practical terms:

> *Extreme life is personal friendship with God, peace in my soul, and the practice of transformational community, where together we worship God and live to serve one another and change our world.*

Tell me, is real life inside the matrix, in what's beamed into your mind from the outside in? Or, as Gatorade brilliantly advertises, "Is it *in* you?" So *is* it in you? Are you looking for life somewhere around you? For the Jesus-follower, *extreme life is "Christ in you, the hope of glory."*[5] It's the best imaginable life. Or maybe we could say it's the best life you could never imagine, because what Christ has to offer us is infinitely far out of our worldly reality. Imagine: There's a world out there that you can't imagine.

MEGADEATH

A year after Adrien Brody won the Academy Award for Best Actor, my wife and I finally watched *The Pianist,* the gripping story of the Polish musician Wladyslaw Szpilman, who somehow managed to survive the holocaust. A masterful pianist—and a Jew—Szpilman lived and nearly died in Warsaw during the Second World War. His life was a leaf in a five-year hurricane of unspeakable suffering.

As you watch the film, you are gripped by the confusion, uncertainty, and terror of Szpilman and his family as the Nazi death machine carefully disguises their "final solution" to the "Jewish problem." It's a fact of history that most of the Jews who died in Hitler's pogroms (a Yiddish word that means "devastation") didn't have a clue they were going to be killed until the moment their executioners released poisonous gas in the "showers" of the death camps.

I'm haunted by many images from *The Pianist,* but one in particular, a turning point in the story, gave me a deep sense of despair. After the Jewish population was relocated to a few square blocks of old Warsaw, Szpilman watches from a window as bricklayers construct a wall across a narrow street, imprisoning the *Juden* in what would become known as the Warsaw Ghetto.

As that wall rises slowly—one row of bricks and then another—you have the sense that it represents the end of hope. The fate of thousands is now sealed and certain. Life will go on in the Ghetto's narrow streets and dark buildings, but not for long.

> They are the gatekeepers. They are guarding all the doors. They are holding all the keys, which means that sooner or later, someone is going to have to fight them.
> —Morpheus

This isn't really happening.

It is.

Sometime soon this will be over.

It won't.

They really aren't doing this to us.

They are.

No human beings could do these kinds of things to other human beings.

They could. And they do.

It couldn't get any worse than this.

It could. It will.

Someone will surely rescue us.

They won't.

Certainly, someone in the world cares.

If they do, they aren't here.

It's now just a matter of time.

Only Szpilman and a handful of others will survive. Maybe only Szpilman.

GERMANS AND EGYPTIANS

The Warsaw Ghetto was a replay of another time in Hebrew history. *The Pianist* says nothing about this, but I wonder how many of the Jews trapped in Warsaw thought about their forebears enslaved in Egypt, living a life of depravation as if there were no other. I wonder how many Polish Jews imagined those redbrick walls, like the Red Sea, collapsing in a moment of divine intervention. I can't imagine they *didn't* imagine those things, especially each spring as many of them celebrated Passover.

The film passes over those religious elements as if they were not, are not, a factor. For many Jews today, in fact, God is history, because the suffering of the holocaust was so horrific. Their reasonable question is this: If there is a God, and he's the God of Israel, how could he have been silent for some of the worst years in human history? Why did he do *nothing*?

I'm certainly not in a position to make a judgment about this, but may I suggest this thought: If the holocaust has become a reason for millions of people not to believe in God, it certainly is a reason to believe in hell. It shows us how a godless world can cave in on itself like a poorly engineered cesspool. This is why the Crucifixion was so dreadful; it was extreme because human darkness is extreme.

> Without knowing it, we were lackeys of the devil. What felt like freedom was bondage.
> —John Piper

Life without God is a ghetto of the dying. Pretending it isn't, pretending it will get better, even living like everything is normal, doesn't make it so—this won't change reality. Human life is as bold and as brittle as the towers of the World Trade Center, another reminder of the fragility of humankind's highest achievements. Even as we mourn the astounding loss of life and honor the memory of those who gave their lives to save others, we acknowledge that the WTC was a twenty-first-century Tower of Babel.[6]

Life in a dying world is an oxymoron, but we live like we're not dying. We're walled in on every side, but we go on believing there is no world beyond the one we know. It's *The Truman Show,* life in a giant bubble.

The Warsaw Ghetto was a world of extreme death. The Cross is an exit from the darkness of my selfishness and sin and an entry point into God's world of extreme life. Cross-followers are "a people belonging to God" who declare the praises of him who called them "out of darkness into his wonderful light."[7] The Cross takes on the walls . . . and takes them down. This text has meant so much to me for so many reasons: "He himself [Christ] is our peace, who has . . . destroyed the barrier, the dividing wall of hostility."[8]

The walls, of course, aren't made of literal bricks and mortar. Nor are they around us, or at the end of the road ahead of us. The walls are in me. Are they *in* you? Our problem is with walls in our hearts. Walls of hostility keeping us away from God. Barricades on the pathway of life. Shattered glass is scattered in the street between my house and yours, and both of us are barefoot.

At this point, let me talk about some of the common elements of life in the new millennium that are making it increasingly difficult to know God and fully experience extreme life. Keep in mind (and I'll keep reminding you) that taking up your cross is the only way to get over the broken glass, through the wall, and out of the ghetto.

RAMPANT INDIVIDUALISM

So why are things the way they are? Why do all of us feel so imprisoned? Why do God and his extreme life seem so inaccessible? As I see it, more than anything else, the problem in our world is rampant individualism: "Experts searching for a cause [for our rising levels of hostility in America] blame an increasing sense of self-importance, the widespread feeling that things should happen my way."[9]

In the words of Scott Russell Sanders:

> Individualism dead-ends in loneliness.
> —Paul Wadell

The cult of the individual shows up everywhere in American lore, which celebrates drifters, rebels, and loners, while pitying or reviling the pillars of the community. The backwoods explorer like Daniel Boone, the riverboat rowdy like Mike Fink, the lumberjack, the prospector, the rambler and the gambler, the daring crook like Jesse James and the resourceful killer like Billy the Kid, along with countless lonesome cowboys, all wander, unattached, through the greatest spaces of our imagination.

When society begins to close in, making demands and asking questions, our heroes hit the road. Like Huckleberry Finn, they are forever lighting out for the Territory, where nobody will tell them what to do. Huck Finn ran away from what he called civilization in order to leave behind the wickedness of slavery, and who can blame him, but he was also running away from church and school and neighbors, from aunts who made him wash before meals, from girls who cramped his style, from chores, from gossip, from the whole nuisance of living alongside other people.[10]

And it's getting worse. According to the findings of Robert Putnam, published in his widely acclaimed *Bowling Alone,* the younger the person, the less he or she is committed to groups, politics, church, or clubs.[11] This social research shows dramatically the unraveling of community and social order on the one hand, and the corresponding rise of narcissism on the other. Sociologists have suggested a number of key factors in the decline of our interest in one another.

OBSESSED WITH THE FRONTIER

First, we are restless. Way back in 1849, Scottish journalist Alexander MacKay wrote, "How readily an American makes up his mind to try his fortunes elsewhere." The "M-factor"—movement, migration, and mobility—it's what's shaped our national character. As Americans, we've even found a direct relationship between mobility and success. You gotta move to get a better job.

But mobility is an enemy of friendship. As a direct result of mobility, we Americans have learned how to make friends quickly . . . and leave them behind just as quickly, something Alvin Toffler calls "modular relationships." You've heard the term "throwaway generation"? Toffler coined that term too. What is less known is his parallel expression, "throwaway relationship." We plug in and then unplug from friends and family, spouse and children, often with little regard for the consequences for the ones we love. Putnam writes, "People who expect to move in the next five years are 20–25 percent less likely to attend church . . . volunteer, or work on community projects than those who expect to stay put."[12]

This month, at our church, we did a survey of people who fell out of our giving records. We wanted to know how many families had stopped supporting the church over the previous twelve months and why. We identified over one hundred households, and when we made phone calls, we discovered a number of them had moved and one out of four had a new phone number—25 percent in a single year!

> We seek our own private life, with a private house, a private car, a private office, and not content with that, we want within our home a private room, a private telephone, a private television, and so on. Once we have attained that, and systematically undercut many of our interdependencies with other people, then we wonder why we are lonely.
> —Elaine Storkey, *The Search for Intimacy*

Here in the greater Phoenix area, people are especially mobile—just about everyone is from somewhere else. I'm from Ohio. My wife is from California. And our three kids, all born in Arizona, now live in California, and my daughter and her husband are considering a move to Colorado. To each his own! And that's part of the problem.

My family name, Kinnaman, traces its roots to Colonial America, and, for nearly two hundred years, home was Ohio. Not anymore. My dad was one of those young men who went west and never went back. We love our freedom, but sadly we love it more than friends and family, and people everywhere are paying the price of loneliness. I have great respect for several families in our church who have determined not to move, who have turned down lucrative promotions, because of the spiritual and relational downside of relocating.

It happens all the time. Just this week a younger man in my church, whom I thought would be with us for life, asked to get together with me to process a decision he has to make regarding a significant promotion offer from his firm.

"Much better pay," he told me, "but we'll have to move."

"Not you!" I lamented. I wanted to say, *"Et tu, Bruté?"* It's a very tough decision, because the new position will take him away from the place he and his extended family have lived his entire life. Consider this: "From one man he [God] made every nation of men, that they should inhabit the whole earth; and he determined the times set for them and *the exact places* where they should live."[13]

There's something to be said about staying put,[14] but our world mercilessly and relentlessly entices us with "better opportunities." I know this sounds upside-down, but mobility is often the illusion of freedom. Freedom is not necessarily found in moving on. (Is it *in* you?) More often than not, I need to put my restlessness on the Cross, because more often than not the Cross is going to tell me to stay put.

TELEVISION FOR LIFE

The *second* factor in our declining interest in one another and our inclining love of self is *technology, mass media, mostly TV*. Even though the Web has made our world smaller and technology in many ways has made our lives better, we all pretty much know that we're becoming more and more isolated, even less human. For a preview of a possible future, watch *The Matrix*.

> [Television] is a medium of entertainment which permits millions of people to listen to the same joke at the same time, and yet remain lonesome.
> —T. S. Eliot

Reading Putnam's findings about the impact of television blew me away. Studies have found that TV is literally mindless, that it has a mesmerizing effect on the human brain. According to Putnam, television absorbed 40 percent of the average American's free time in 1995. Between 1965 and 1995 we gained an average of six hours a week in leisure time, but we've devoted almost all of that to watching more TV.

Never again will I be able to accept "I'm too busy" as an excuse from anybody in my church. Everyone, it seems, has time for television, but not for one another, not for the things that matter. Consider the impact that would be made if every adult in a church of five hundred gave just two hours a week to volunteering in the community (only a fraction of the hours per week people watch television). That would be roughly 50,000 hours of community service a year . . . just from one congregation! Or if all those people got a minimum-wage, part-time, two-hour-a-week job, and gave the money away, it would amount to around $300,000 annually for charity! If ten million American Christians did that, it would raise a whopping $6 *billion*—on top of what everyone is already giving!

But these things aren't important to us; TV is our God. Even the most faithful church people, on average, spend far more time watching TV than attending services or Bible studies. And we wonder why we don't know God very well, and why, instead of experiencing extreme life, we are extremely stressed.

Consider what lots of TV time will do for you and your family. According to Putnam,

- Husbands and wives spend three to four times as much time watching TV together as they spend talking to each other.

- Couples spend six to seven times as much time watching TV as they spend participating in church and community activities outside their home.

- More and more of our TV viewing is alone, with less than 5 percent of teens watching with their parents.

- In the evening Americans, above all else, watch TV.

- The more people watch TV, the less they volunteer.

> The world, the media, they *devalue* all the things I value.
> —Donna Otto

- The more people watch TV, the less they write letters to friends and family.

- The more people watch TV, the less they participate in clubs and group activities.

- The more people watch TV, the less they attend church.

- The more people watch TV, the less likely they are to work on a community project and the more likely they are to flip off another driver.

- The more people watch TV, the less they feel good about themselves.[15]

For years one major cable provider had a little jingle: *Now you're livin'!*[16] What's that supposed to mean? That you'll encounter and experience extreme life with extreme 100-channel cable TV? That's livin'? To me, that much TV will ensure you die a slow mental and spiritual death. TV is the principal symbol and propagator of the god-less world around us. TV is a gargantuan toilet that flushes godlessness right into your soul. Thousands of years before television, King David wrote,

> I will be careful to lead a blameless life. . . . I will walk in my house with blameless heart. I will set before my eyes no vile thing. The deeds of faithless men I hate; they will not cling to me.

> PSALM 101:2–3

Here's something to remember:

PUT GOD FIRST AND TURN OFF YOUR TELEVISION.

STUFFMART

The *third* factor contributing to the decline in our interest in one another, *the third log on the fire of self-interest, is consumerism.* Consumerism is the unholy matrimony between the advertising industry and our common misbelief that getting more things will make us happier.

"Oh . . . I so need that!"

Au contraire. Did you know that product sales depend on creating a sense of need in the consumer, a sense of *unhappiness?* Unhappiness is the engine of our consumer-driven world, which perpetuates the illusion that things will make you happy! Is that ludicrous or what? When I talk about the Cross, about how that you have to die to live, most good Americans (and many good American Christians) will stare at me with glazed eyes.

In the mass deception of the cult of the individual, the idea of giving up and giving in is unthinkable. It *seems* backward, which is why Paul says the Cross is foolishness to the world.[17] But try to turn your brain around for a moment. Think with me. The Cross is backward thinking . . . but consumerism isn't? *Advertisers create the illusion of depravation in a nation that already accounts for 50 percent of the world's consumption, a nation that has less than 5 percent of the world's population.*

As you sit there in front of your plasma-screen TV (which you had to have to make you happy), you know you have more than you need (and, thus, you didn't really need the new TV). But innumerable advertisers will tell you, in countless hellishly clever ways, why you need what they have to sell and why you'll have residual unhappiness if you don't make the purchase.

I think the classic commercial in this regard is the guy sitting at the dinner table with his wife and kids (now that's an anachronism!) with a toy car stuck on his head. The announcer says something like this: "Tom has a new car on his mind. Buy the new car, Tom. Buy the new car." Between the lines we can hear the devil's voice: *The restlessness in your soul won't go away, Tom, until you buy that car. Buy the car, Tom. You'll be happy. You deserve it.*

Man, have I ever heard that voice. And weeks, or sometimes only days later, I'm on to something else I think will make me happy. Confessing my own sin, I've found that the Internet is an endless source of things I never knew I needed. It's a fact that advertising contributes to the high levels of anxiety among Americans. Like I said, we consume a whopping 50 percent of the world's natural resources *and* probably 90 percent of the world's antidepressants.[18]

THINKING BACKWARD DIFFERENTLY

Doug Glynn, our young adults pastor, is a huge Minnesota Vikings fan. Last season . . . I think it was last season (if I were a Vikings fan, I'd remember) . . . maybe it was two years ago . . . Doug had a church meeting that conflicted with a televised Vikings game . . . and I can't remember why me, but Doug asked me to tape the game . . . which I did. *And he passionately insisted that I keep the outcome a secret.*

I'm *not* a Vikings fan, but I kept an eye on the game. And the Vikings got crushed. I mean, it was, like, 56 to 3.[19] It had to be one of their worst games ever. Half an hour or so after it ended, *Ding, dong*. There's Doug at my front door asking for the video. So what am I going to tell him?

I couldn't decide if I should be his friend and give him the tape, or his pastor and tell him that his best friend just died. He'd be better off not watching how his buddy got killed, you know.

When Doug saw my face, he knew I wanted to say something about the outcome, and he literally screamed at me, his pastor, his boss, *"DON'T TELL ME WHAT HAPPENED!!!"*

He told me the next day, though, that my face said it all. I mean, how can you keep something like that out of your eyes? I never gave him the score, but he knew, *he just knew,* his Vikings had lost.

So don't you just hate it when people do things like that? Or when they tell you exactly what happens in a movie before you get to see it? Or give away the ending of a good book? Well, the Bible is different. The Bible is definitely a book where you want to know as soon as possible how the story ends, because the story of the Bible is your story.

Ironically, in order to discover the meaning of life, you have to start at the end of the story: You have to think backward. *To be for-ward-thinking you have to be backward-looking,* and how you look will determine how you live. Reality isn't just what you see.

Your worldview is the way you understand life and how it works, and that's how you live. It's the simple, timeless proverb: "The fear of the LORD is the beginning of wisdom."[20] God is the starting point, and *wisdom* in Hebrew simply means "life-skill," that is, how wisely or skillfully you live out your life. Here's what Jesus said about this:

> The eye is the lamp of the body. If your eyes are good, your whole body will be full of light. But if your eyes are bad [if you don't see straight], your whole body will be full of dark-ness. If then the light within you is darkness, how great is that darkness!
>
> MATTHEW 6:22–23

LIFE TO DIE FOR

Taking up your cross is backward thinking, it's a way of looking at life that turns you right-side-up. The message of the Cross, though, is more than a principle, more than a different way to think. I keep emphasizing this: Coming to the Cross takes us way beyond the routines of good religion and solid living to a point of discovery, of encounter, of transformation. The Cross takes us out of our small, confined, self-enclosed world into the bright realty of Christ-life.

Jesus spoke of the journey of life this way:

> If anyone would come after me, he must deny himself and take up his cross and follow me. For whoever wants to save his life will lose it, but whoever loses his life for me will find it. What good will it be for a man if he gains the whole world, yet forfeits his soul? Or what can a man give in exchange for his soul?
>
> MATTHEW 16:24–26

This is backward thinking. This is extreme. This is living life in a way that's fundamentally contrary to what we've always thought about happiness and peace. Everything in my soul screams in protest, "The path to life is *not* death!" . . . but as long I scream, I can't hear the truth. I can't hear Jesus insisting that "anyone who does not carry his cross and follow me cannot be my disciple."[21]

It's almost incomprehensible that carrying a cross, something so painful and burdensome, would lighten the load of my life. Oddly enough, however, carrying your cross is essentially about giving your burdens to Christ, who promised, "Come to me, all you who are weary and burdened, and I will give you rest. Take my yoke upon you and learn from me, for I am gentle and humble in heart, and you will find rest for your souls. [Imagine this, believe this, experience this:] *For my yoke is easy and my burden is light.*" (Matthew 11:28–30, emphasis mine)

The benefits of taking up your cross are extreme. Coming to the cross, taking it up, carrying it on the journey, releases the power of God in your life to do things humanly impossible. This is extreme life: graciously enduring a difficult relationship. Working faithfully in a less than perfect job. Releasing yourself and others from the curse of unforgiveness. Getting past your past. Making every moment of your life count, and loving it. Helping others to experience the God who is transforming you.

Again, something deep inside all of us resists the way of the Cross. We're obsessed with individualism, and we insist on living in the ghetto of our private, self-serving, self-defined life. All the while the world around us keeps piling on the illusion that living for yourself is the path to happiness.

JESUS ON CONSUMERISM

How you look at things will determine how you look at things. Get it? How you think about possessions will determine what you do with those possessions and what those possessions will do to you. Are they *in* you? Jesus said,

> Do not store up for yourselves treasures on earth, where
> moth and rust destroy, and where thieves break in and steal.
> But store up for yourselves treasures in heaven, where moth
> and rust do not destroy, and where thieves do not break in
> and steal. For where your treasure is, there your heart will be
> also.
>
> MATTHEW 6:19–21

The Greek term for *destroy* means "wipe out." Natural and human causes will eventually eliminate everything we treasure on earth. A few years ago *Time* featured a foldout aerial panorama of an upscale middle-America neighborhood (in Oklahoma) devastated by a tornado of historic proportions.

When I first saw the scene, it took my breath away. Everything was literally *wiped out*—it looked like the old black and white photos of Hiroshima after the A bomb. The devastation was so extreme that the only way people who lived in this neighborhood could find their homes was by looking for the house number painted on the curb.

You see, possessions give us a false sense of security. Jesus warned, "Watch out! Be on your guard against all kinds of greed; a man's life does not consist in the abundance of his possessions." And he then told this parable:

> The ground of a certain rich man produced a good crop. He
> thought to himself, "What shall I do? I have no place to store
> my crops." Then he said, "This is what I'll do. I will tear
> down my barns and build bigger ones, and there I will store

all my grain and my goods. And I'll say to myself, 'You have plenty of good things laid up for many years. Take life easy; eat, drink and be merry.'"

But God said to him, "You fool! This very night your life will be demanded from you. Then who will get what you have prepared for yourself?" This is how it will be with anyone who stores up things for himself but is not rich toward God.

LUKE 12:15–21

The illusion is that possessions will make me happy, and if I end up with a lottery of possessions, I will be *extremely* happy. But possessions steal my heart away from God and are so self-serving that they inevitably hinder my relationships with others and weaken my ability to love. Just think what happens when we have a lot of money, a lot of stuff:

- We have to protect it.

- We have to be secretive about it.

- We get upset if others steal it or abuse it. Like if I let someone stay at my house—or drive my car—and they don't take care of it exactly as I would.

- If we have less stuff than others, it makes us covetous, angry, envious.

- How much money we have even determines what kind of people we hang out with. People almost always are best friends with other people who have about the same income and social status. Who are your friends? You probably don't often hang out with people who have a lot more or a lot less. Amazing! Money sets the boundaries for friendships and even marriage and family.

- The number one cause of divorce is conflict over money. *More than problems with sex!*

EXTREME ANXIETY

Don't you feel your anxiety level rising just reading through that list? Money and possessions absolutely affect how we feel about ourselves and how we relate to others. Doug Pagitt tells this story on himself in LEADERSHIP:

> It was in the back of a bus in Guatemala, sitting with six people. . . .
>
> All of us were living off of "just barely enough." Here we were, in a terribly poor part of a poor country, building houses for the poorest people, talking about how hard it is to live on what we all make.
>
> We were college graduates, and teachers, and building contractors, and we concluded that we didn't make enough money. I began to see it clearly: We were all stuck in a consumerist mindset. Our coffee shop and restaurant expenses alone would build housing for the people of this village, if we simply lived on less.
>
> For that cause, I am willing to confront the person who says he can't give, but who has a car, a cable subscription, and thousands of dollars in credit-card debt, with the need for a new attitude toward money. Once you start tithing, you soon realize you can live off 90 percent. It's really a shift in thinking: If I have a dollar, I don't have to spend 100 pennies. I can spend 90, and that's still a lot.[22]

Certainly it is impossible to eradicate injustice, to equalize perfectly everything in our unequal world. Yet is it possible that no property can be acquired except with some element of injustice? To own something (and I own a lot of things) might mean that someone, somewhere in the world, maybe just a couple miles from my home, will have less than he needs to live. Randy Alcorn develops this theme in his extraordinary book *Money, Possessions, and Eternity:*

> Materialism treats the temporal as if it were eternal and the eternal as if it were nonexistent. It is the inevitable consequence of atheism or agnosticism and invariably leads to the elevation of things on the one hand and the depreciation of people on the other. . . .
>
> Materialism will inevitably produce the kind of society

increasingly evident in America—a society of individualism, where people live parallel lives, not meaningfully intersecting with others. A society where independence is the only absolute, where self-interest is the only creed, where convenience and expediency and profitability are the only values. A society where people know the price of everything, but the value of nothing—where people have a great deal to live on, but very little to live for.[23]

Possessions make me happy for a moment, but not forever—sometimes not even for a few days. It's weird how getting stuff only makes you want more stuff. Possessions possess us, because they have an unusual power over us, which in some cases might even be demon power. I touched on this in an earlier chapter, that the term *mammon* as Jesus uses it[24] was understood as the name of an actual spiritual being, a dark angel of materialism.

> In Western society today the fundamental value of anything is determined economically. . . . Consumerism is a gospel, and it tells us we are liberated through what we own, not through intimate relationships, and that our identity is measured by our possessions, not by the richness of our lives. . . . Consumerism and materialism are lethal for friendships because good and lasting friendships are possible only with people who are able to be content and satisfied with other people, but the last thing our consumerist culture wants is for us to be content with anything.
> —Paul Wadell, *Becoming Friends*

The *Theological Dictionary of the New Testament* tells us, "Because of the demonic power inherent in possessions, surrender to them brings practical enslavement."[25] Randy Alcorn adds,

Satan is the Lord of Materialism. "Mammon" is but an alias of the Prince of Darkness, who has vested interests in whether or not we understand and obey Christ's commands concerning our money and possessions. . . . What we do with our money loudly affirms which kingdom we belong to.[26]

Certainly, our possessions are gifts from God, but God doesn't give us stuff simply to make us happy, and extreme life is not measured by an abundance of possessions. Ultimately, God gives us everything as a test of who we really are, and he's watching to see what we'll do with what he gives us. Jesus, on the cross, says, "Give it back. Give it up. Give it away."

Someday God may not only ask you to give up one of your three meals a day so that someone else can have one, but it's conceivable he might ask you to give up your only meal. At the risk of your own life. So that someone else can live one *more* day. A mother would do this for her child. The Cross says that Jesus would do it for us.

The life of God is a river that runs through it, fresh in, fresh out, not a poisoned, odorous sea of salt and death. We think possessions will make us happy now, but God wants us to give money and possessions away to prepare us for eternity. We measure the value of our lives and the lives of others based on what we have; God measures the value of our lives based on what we've given away. God's Son, Jesus, set that standard.

I own nothing. God owns everything. I'm only a steward, a banker, holding in trust something that belongs to someone else. People value what they become—their own success—and the possessions they have acquired. God values what people have done to serve *others* to make *them* successful.

Thinking backward is starting with the end of the story, letting eternity shape your time instead of letting your time shape your eternity. The more you can think backward, the more freely you can move forward. And here is the most extreme kind of thinking in the universe: Don't live to make money and buy things, live to serve others with whatever God gives you, because giving is the *only* way you can

- lay up treasure in heaven;

- keep treasures on earth from demonizing you;

- keep your life completely open with God;

- keep all your stuff from interfering in your relationships with others.

If you want out of the dark ghetto, you have to think backward, live backward. *You have to take up your cross. You have to die to live.*

Viewpoint #6:
The Cross is the portal to extreme life.

SCRIPTURE

†6M "He [Christ] redeemed us in order that the blessing given to Abraham might come to the Gentiles through Christ Jesus, so that by faith we might receive the promise of the Spirit."[27]

†6Tu "We know that our old self was crucified with him so that the body of sin might be done away with, that we should no longer be slaves to sin—because anyone who has died has been freed from sin. Now if we died with Christ, we believe that we will also live with him."[28]

†6W "Surely he took up our infirmities and carried our sorrows, yet we considered him stricken by God, smitten by him, and afflicted. But he was pierced for our transgressions, he was crushed for our iniquities; the punishment that brought us peace was upon him, and by his wounds we are healed."[29]

†6Th "He himself bore our sins in his body on the tree, so that we might die to sins and live for righteousness; by his wounds you have been healed. For you were like sheep going astray, but now you have returned to the Shepherd and Overseer of your souls."[30]

†6F "The other criminal rebuked him [the first criminal]. 'Don't you fear God,' he said, 'since you are under the same sentence? We are punished justly, for we are getting what our deeds deserve. But this man has done nothing wrong.' Then he said, 'Jesus, remember me when you come into your kingdom.' Jesus answered him, *'I tell you the truth, today you will be with me in paradise.'*"[31]

†6Sa "When evening came, many who were demon-possessed were brought to him, and he drove out the spirits with a word and healed all the sick. This was to fulfill what was spoken

through the prophet Isaiah: 'He took up our infirmities and carried our diseases.'"[32]

†6Su "Jesus said to her [Martha], 'I am the resurrection and the life. He who believes in me will live, even though he dies; and whoever lives and believes in me will never die. Do you believe this?'"[33]

CHAPTER ELEVEN

Beyond Extreme Life

Viewpoint #7:
The Cross is the portal to eternal life with God.

Dead.

The word has a feel all its own.

"Cancer" is bad enough, but "dead" is the end.

It's a word so charged with emotion and fear that we only use it for people we don't know, like, "The morgue is filled with dead people." Or, "This is a photo of war dead war."

In many cemeteries of the War Between the States, you'll find these words:

Glory guards with solemn rounds
The bivouac of the dead.
——Theodore O'Hara, "Bivouac of the Dead"

Dead. Dead guys. The dead.

When my father died, I never referred to him as *dead*. "Gone" is okay. Or "his life ended." Or, "he's not living." Or, "my father passed away." But never *dead*. "Dead" is such an impersonal word. And it's so final.

Human life was not created to die. Certainly, few living things, if any, want to die, try to die, but human beings not only die, they think about dying. And about what dying means. Everyone, it seems, has a fear of death to one degree or another. Some may call death an adventure, an opportunity, a door to the future, but whatever we call it, we'd rather not go there until the very last possible moment. If heaven is our home, why do we feel so much more at home here?

I think often about my father. How much he loved life. How his soul was filled with music and art and clever, creative energy. He especially loved classical music, woodworking, and trains. And he was nuts about Arizona—he loved our vast deserts, purple canyons, blue-green mountains of Ponderosa pine. When I listen to classical music, I think of him and wonder, "Dad, are you missing this? Do you still have this? Is there music in heaven? Did you get a new table saw?"

Though we imagine these things, no one really knows life-after-death details, the fine print of eternal life. A year ago my son David did a national study on what people believe about life after death.[1] A popular Web site[2] picked up his story, and the day they released it, the server in the Barna offices crashed, overloaded with tens of thousands of hits. People are dying to know what happens in the next life.

As I said, all of us to some degree fear death, and if we don't fear it, we simply don't want life to end. I mean, how many people *like* caskets and cemeteries? In *Further Along the Road Less Traveled*, M. Scott Peck remarks to one of his patients, "You really do have quite a fear of death." The gentleman insists, "No, no, no, I'm not afraid to die. It's just those damn hearses and funeral parlors that bother me."[3]

We laugh about death, but our humor is a front, a blind, a pretense. Fact is, death is something no one likes to face, and because we don't like to face it, we really don't know how to deal with it when it comes. When the doctor told our family that my dad was going to die, we all sat there in frozen silence. A few minutes later we were all in my dad's room telling him. Everyone broke down and sobbed, except my dad, who said gruffly, "What are you all crying for? I'm not dead yet."

In this chapter I want to face off with four important questions:

- Why does death seem like a mystery?

- What happens when death remains a mystery?

- How can we take some of the mystery out of death, and with it the fear?

- What happens, practically speaking, when death becomes less of a mystery to us and loses its sting?

THE MYSTERY

Why does death seem like a mystery? I have a simple answer: our ignorance. This isn't meant to be a slam on anyone. It's just that death is a mystery because we know so little about it until we die. Furthermore, our understanding about death is distorted by at least two things: *humanism,* or the "natural" view of death without any consideration of its spiritual implications, and our *contemporary, deathless world.*

My mother's father was a country pastor. At the end of a dusty road in Michigan (my mother thought it was the end of the world), stood St. Stephen Lutheran Church, steeple tall and bright white against a background of emerald summer trees. Former members were gathered around that little church in the "congregation of the dead." My mother remembers playing on the headstones.

> My romance with death has given me a sense of the meaningfulness of this life.
> —M. Scott Peck

She remembers, too, bodies of family members lying in state in the parlors of country homes; it was even fashionable to photograph them in peaceful repose. I just happened to see (online) an old sepia picture of aged Civil War veterans standing proudly behind the very open casket (not even sure if it was a casket, exactly) of a deceased comrade. I've done dozens of funerals, but that antique photo of a well-dressed dead man still got my attention.

Today, though, death is sterile. Dying in rest homes and hospitals, the bodies of the elderly vanish in the night, transported to morgues and mortuaries in unmarked vans. For many, death is only as real as a movie. By contrast, my lovely cousin Kathy is an ophthalmologist who got her start working with organ donations, specifically corneas. You know where they get those, don't you? From cadavers. So she had a key to the morgue, and just about any time, day or night (people don't die on schedule), she'd go down there and "harvest" corneas.

I know: You don't want to think about this stuff. It's morbid. It's also less culturally acceptable to look death in the corneas and pause to ponder what it means for life. Hans Küng writes, "What in the Middle Ages was known as the *ars moriendi,* the 'art of dying,' is something for which our society has not developed any sort of cultural background."[4]

Very simply, we don't talk about death, and we don't know how to die. A few years ago when I gave a series of talks at church on death and dying, a friend asked me frantically, "How long are we going to be talking about this subject?" Well, for a whole three weeks—three weeks in ten years of sermons! I think a lot of people were grateful and relieved when I followed up with a series on *money*!

> We must all become familiar with the thought of death if we want to grow into really good people.
> —Albert Schweitzer

SOME THINGS ARE *NOT* BETTER LEFT UNSAID

Second question: *What happens when death remains a mystery?* Another simple answer: fear. Our cultural setting is so different from that of the Bible, where death was as real as life, especially for people whose baptism certificate could be a ticket to "sporting events" at the Coliseum. It was a world we can't imagine, so we don't understand deeply what Scripture teaches us about death, and, of course, what we don't understand, we fear. Ignorance goes hand in hand with superstition and dread; as a result, we have lost the "art of dying."

Touring funeral homes, visiting cemeteries, and reading books like this, however, don't make the fear go away, because *the fear of death, inherent in human life, is universal.* Ernest Becker, in his Pulitzer Prize-winning book *The Denial of Death,* writes,

> There are "healthy-minded" persons who maintain that fear of death is not a natural thing for man, that we are not born with it. An increasing number of careful studies on how the actual fear of death develops in the child agree fairly well that the child has no knowledge of death until about the age of three to five. . . .
>
> This theory puts the whole burden of anxiety onto the child's nurture and not his nature. . . . But there is another side. A large body of people would agree . . . that nevertheless, the fear of death is natural and is present in everyone, that it is the basic fear that influences all [other fears], a fear from which no one is immune, no matter how disguised it may be. [The pragmatist] William James spoke very early for this school [of thought], and with his usual colorful realism he called death "the worm at the core of man's pretensions to happiness."[5]

LOVING FUNERALS

I'm also persuaded that *the universal fear of death points to God, that there is a God.* If it doesn't "prove" there's a God, it certainly gets people thinking in God's direction. Years ago another young pastor and I were standing in a lobby prior to a funeral. It was, like always, deathly quiet; everyone was whispering (which, actually, often makes me want to laugh out loud). My friend leaned into my ear and hissed with hot breath, "I *love* to do funerals." I thought for a moment I detected a Transylvanian accent. Just the way he said "love" gave me chills. I knew he wasn't joking, though, when he repeated himself: "I love to do funerals . . . *because the needs are so great and people are so open to God.*" Now I *love* to do funerals too, because of the opportunities they afford me to speak of the God I love.

Human beings have a strange abhorrence of death and dead bodies. To me, our fear of death is a primal witness to our origin as creatures of a Divine Being. Our aversion to death suggests we were destined for immortality—something in every human soul objects to death and wants to live forever. People die, but they shouldn't die. Why? Because *we were created for eternity.*

Jonathan Edwards, considered by some to be the greatest theologian in American history, once wrote:

> Death, with the pains and agonies with which it is usually brought on, is not merely a limiting of existence, but is a most terrible calamity; and to such a creature as man, capable of conceiving of immortality, and made with so earnest a desire after it, and capable of foresight and of reflection on approaching death, and that has such an extreme dread of it, is a calamity above all others terrible. . . . It is [clear] that mankind were not originally subjected to this calamity.[6]

Robert Morey said, "Death tears man in half. *Man was made to live, not die.*"[7]

UNLOCKING THE MYSTERY

Third question: *How can we take some of the mystery out of death, and with it the fear?* By turning to the Bible, the Christian view of life and death, and, specifically, to the death and resurrection of Christ. *The Cross is a portal through the dark walls of death to resurrection and eternal life.* Perhaps there is no more illuminating passage about death and life than Paul's famous essay on the final resurrection:

> Listen, I tell you a mystery: We will not all sleep, but we will all be changed—in a flash, in the twinkling of an eye, at the last trumpet. For the trumpet will sound, the dead will be raised imperishable, and we will be changed. For the perishable must clothe itself with the imperishable, and the mortal with immortality. When the perishable has been clothed with the imperishable, and the mortal with immortality, then the saying that is written will come true: "Death has been swallowed up in victory."
>
> *Where, O death, is your victory?*
> *Where, O death, is your sting?*
>
> The sting of death is sin, and the power of sin is the law. But thanks be to God! He gives us the victory through our Lord Jesus Christ.
>
> 1 CORINTHIANS 15:51–57, EMPHASIS MINE

When Christ died on the cross, he overcame the power of sin, which is death, and God the Father affirmed his finished work by raising him from the dead, "the firstfruits of those who have fallen asleep."[8]

"Therefore, my dear brothers," Paul concludes, "stand firm. Let nothing move you. Always give yourselves fully to the work of the Lord, because you know that your labor in the Lord is not in vain."[9] Paul's "therefore," his brief summary, shows us how the death and resurrection of Christ impacted his life—and, certainly, the lives of the other apostles as well. Essentially, for the apostles, the fear of death was a non-factor in life, because each of them (except John), including Paul, died a martyr's death, some unspeakably hideous.

Whatever might be said among historians about whether or not Jesus was raised from the dead (I certainly believe he was), the fact remains that *something* so extraordinary happened to the Savior that his closest friends—who had previously run away and abandoned him because of fear—were now willing to give their lives. Nor was it just a matter of love and devotion to their leader; many men have done that. No, they willingly died because of their core belief in what Christ did through his death and resurrection. They didn't just die for a cause, or even for a friend: They died for the message of the Cross and the hope of the Resurrection.

Paul is very clear on this:

> If Christ has not been raised, your faith is futile; you are still in your sins. Then those also who have fallen asleep in Christ are lost. If only for this life we have hope in Christ, we are to be pitied more than all men.
>
> 1 CORINTHIANS 15:17–19

FUNERALS FROM HELL

Becoming a Christ-follower doesn't include an exemption from physical death, but it dulls the edge of the fear of death. Knowing Christ does not take away the sorrow of losing someone you love, but it takes away the finality and hopelessness of physical death. I've done two kinds of funerals: One for Christians, the other for non-

Christians. You couldn't tell the difference in the format, in the order of service, but just about anyone can *feel* the difference. I've done services for godly people who lost their lives under awful circumstances, but to everyone's surprise the celebration of their life was filled with inexpressible joy at a service to acknowledge their death.

On the other hand, I've done really sad funerals. Not because the person died tragically or because it was a little girl killed in a go-cart accident (which really happened). Yes, those things are terribly sad, but probably the saddest service I've ever done was for a young man who killed himself. Maybe he killed himself. No one knew for sure, because he died of an overdose. During the service his weeping friends lined up to say a few words about him.

> I will dedicate and sacrifice everything for just a second's worth of how my story's ending. I wish I could know if the direction that I take and all the choices that I make won't end up all for nothing.
> —Hoobastank,
> "Crawling in the Dark"

It was pitiful. Not what they said about him, mind you, but what they tried to say about life and death. No one, it seemed, had a clue. Everyone was desperately trying to say something meaningful, but every comment seemed so superficial. So empty. So hopeless. As I sat there listening, I decided to put aside the notes I'd diligently prepared for the service. "This just won't work here," I told myself, so I took my place behind the podium and passionately shared everything I could about the love of God and the hope he offers us in the death and resurrection of Christ.

M. Scott Peck begins a chapter on the meaning of death with a Carl Sandburg poem titled "Limited":

> I'm riding on a limited express, one of the crack
> trains of the nation.
> Hurtling across the prairie into blue haze and dark air
> go fifteen all-steel coaches holding a thousand people.
> (All the coaches shall be scrap and rust and all the
> men and woman laughing in the diners and
> sleepers shall pass to ashes.)
> I ask a man in the smoker where he is going and he
> answers: "Omaha."[10]

This is—if you couldn't guess—about death. Where are you going? Where's your life going? To Omaha? Jesus has been raised from the dead, and for Christ-followers, our "blessed hope," our future, is the resurrection of our bodies and reunion with those we love:

> The Lord himself will come down from heaven, with a loud command, with the voice of the archangel and with the trumpet call of God, and the dead in Christ will rise first. After that, we who are still alive and are left will be caught up together with them in the clouds to meet the Lord in the air. And so we will be with the Lord forever. [And I love this part:] *"Therefore encourage each other with these words."* [11]

Christian View of Death	*Humanist View of Death*
Death is unnatural.	Death is natural.
Death is a penalty for sin (Romans 5:12).	Death is simply part of life.
Death is a time of sorrow (John 11:33–39).	Death is a time of despair.
Death will be done away with when Christ returns (Revelation 21:4).	Death will always be here.[12]

PRACTICALLY SPEAKING . . .

Fourth question: *What happens, practically speaking, when death becomes less of a mystery to us and loses its sting?* The answer is that we can face death realistically and with little or no fear. I saw that in my father. Man, was he courageous. No, he didn't just walk tall. He couldn't. It wasn't about his posture—it was the positioning of his heart. He never complained, he never cried. Except when his pastor visited him in the hospital and sang a hymn.

My father wasn't just trying to keep a stiff upper lip. He never said anything like "I'm trying to keep a good attitude." He just did. My dad died so well. In many ways, my father taught me more about life in the way he died than in the fifty years I knew him.

> Death is what makes life so meaningful.
> —Orson Wells

King Solomon wrote in his later years, "There is a time for everything, and a season for every activity under heaven: a time to be born and a time to die."[13]

What you believe about death will determine how you live. The Christian meaning of death will give meaning to your life. Death without meaning is life without a purpose.

Viewpoint #7:
The Cross is the portal to eternal life with God.

If you are using these chapter-closing sections as devotionals during the Lenten season, then you know that this is it: This is the last week of Lent, Passion Week, the most significant eight days in human history. Navigate them with thoughtfulness and care.

SCRIPTURE

†7M "If we died with Christ, we believe that we will also live with him. For we know that since Christ was raised from the dead, he cannot die again; death no longer has mastery over him. The death he died, he died to sin once for all; but the life he lives, he lives to God."[14]

†7Tu "Since death came through a man, the resurrection of the dead comes also through a man. For as in Adam all die, so in Christ all will be made alive. But each in his own turn: Christ, the firstfruits; then, when he comes, those who belong to him."[15]

†7W "Then the end will come, when he hands over the kingdom to God the Father after he has destroyed all dominion, authority and power. For he must reign until he has put all his enemies under his feet. The last enemy to be destroyed is death."[16]

†7Th "Do not be ashamed to testify about our Lord, or ashamed of me his prisoner. But join with me in suffering for the gospel, by the power of God, who has saved us and called us to a holy life—not because of anything we have done but because of his own purpose and grace. This grace was given us in Christ Jesus before the beginning of time, but it has now been revealed through the appearing of our Savior, Christ Jesus, who has destroyed death and has brought life and immortality to light through the gospel."[17]

†7F: Good Friday "It is finished."[18]

†7Sa "All things are yours, whether Paul or Apollos or Cephas or the world or life or death or the present or the future—all are yours, and you are of Christ, and Christ is of God."[19]

†7Su: Easter "When the perishable has been clothed with the imperishable, and the mortal with immortality, then the saying that is written will come true: 'Death has been swallowed up in victory.'"

> *Where, O death, is your victory?*
> *Where, O death, is your sting?*

"The sting of death is sin, and the power of sin is the law. But thanks be to God! He gives us the victory through our Lord Jesus Christ. Therefore, my dear brothers, stand firm. Let nothing move you. Always give yourselves fully to the work of the Lord, because you know that your labor in the Lord is not in vain."[20]

PART THREE
Crossways

F—R—E—E—D—O—M!!!

—William Wallace in *Braveheart*

CHAPTER TWELVE

Scandalous Freedom

It is this doctrine, this gospel of Christ crucified, at which the present age, with all its vaunted culture and all its vain philosophies, sneers so broadly.
—Charles Spurgeon

We preach Christ crucified: a stumbling block to Jews and foolishness to Gentiles.
—Paul

The Passion of the Christ was one of the top-grossing films of all time. Within weeks of its release, it was chasing *Lord of the Rings: Return of the King.*

The Cross, though, is a scandal. An outrage.

Scandalous. Outrageous.

Scandalous is still pretty much a negative word, but *outrageous* somehow has come to mean something positive, something excellent, something really cool. Crazy fun. Like the new rocket-fast coasters at

Magic Mountain in Southern California: You could say they're *outrageous*.

Properly, though, outrageous is just as negative as scandalous, as in, I was *outraged* when I heard about a two-year-old boy murdered by his mother's boyfriend, who held him under water in the apartment-complex pool until his little body went limp.

It happened.

It happened to a child in my church just two weeks ago. The funeral was a week ago. (Do you feel outrage?) Then it hit the news that the boyfriend was claiming the child's mother was an accomplice, although there's been no evidence linking her to the crime except his word. Do you believe the testimony of a cold-blooded child-killer? *Scandalous.*

The word *scandal* comes from the Greek term *skandalon,* which refers to something that causes you to trip, "a stumbling block, to be repelled by someone, to take offense," shock and awe, "that which causes revulsion, arouses opposition."[1] *Skandalon* is used in these two verses:

> We preach Christ crucified: *a stumbling block* [*skandalon*] to Jews and foolishness to Gentiles.
>
> 1 CORINTHIANS 1:23, EMPHASIS MINE

> Brothers, if I am still preaching circumcision, why am I still being persecuted? In that case the *offense* [*skandalon*] of the cross has been abolished.
>
> GALATIANS 5:11, EMPHASIS MINE

PRIMAL REVULSION

Certainly *The Passion of the Christ* elicited shock and revulsion. Just today, as my good friend Steve was cutting my hair, the stylist in the next booth overheard us talking about the movie. When she took her fourteen-year-old daughter to see it, she told us, her child couldn't stop weeping. "But did you cry?" I asked. "No," she said, "I got up and walked out a couple times because I couldn't bear to watch the violence."

The scandal of the Cross, though, is *not* in the interminable flogging of Jesus in a bloody R-rated film. *The scandal is in what Jesus taught* (and, indeed, what the Bible teaches) *about the fundamental values of life.* Quite simply, the outrage of the Cross is that so many of the things we value have little or no value. On an even deeper level, the outrage of the Cross is the blessing of dying to yourself.

Perhaps Christ's most significant statement in this regard, one we've visited several times in this book, was this:

> The man who loves his life will lose it, while the man who hates his life in this world will keep it for eternal life.
>
> JOHN 12:25

This is yet another turnout, a viewpoint, a place to stop for a while and meditate. Pause now and ponder. Take a few moments and write down what this statement, so central to the teaching of Jesus, means to you.

Specifically, what elements of your life stand between you and God? Between you and your future? What in your life keeps you from experiencing the deep inner peace you so desperately long for? Or gives you the feeling you are losing your sense of significance? What do you need to lose? In addition to asking yourself, ask other what they thing about your life. Ask your spouse. Ask your best friends.

Dying to self is not simply saying no to that new stereo system you want to put on your credit card. It's not even just saying no to too much alcohol or to illicit sex, although that's certainly a start. Dying to yourself is saying no to what's wrong inside you, even the unforgiveness and rage you feel about "that" person. Another turnout: Stop for a moment and write his/her initials here: _____. Now pray for him/her. It's what Jesus told us to do: "Bless those who curse you, pray for those who mistreat you."[2]

> The outrage of the Cross is that so many of the things we value have little or no value.

Did you see Mel Gibson in *Braveheart*? It's not as hard to watch as *The Passion of the Christ,* but you still want to close your eyes during some of its more brutal moments. Who can forget the final scene, when William Wallace is executed. Putting into the moment everything he's learned in acting class . . . and all his own energy and emotion . . . in defiance of what the world around him stands for . . . in excruciating pain, Mel Gibson screams,

F—R—E—E—D—O—M!

Some things in life are worth dying for, and some things in death are better than life. Living to die, giving up everything to gain everything—this is the scandalous message of the Cross.

A SCANDALOUS CHILD

One of the early Christian communities, the one in the Greek city of Corinth, was in trouble. Reading Paul's first letter to the Corinthians, it's evident they had extraordinary misunderstandings of the essentials of the Christian life, not the least of which was love. Not the love of romance or rhetoric, but the love of self-sacrifice. Love that's more concerned about others than it is about itself. Love that believes all things, hopes all things, endures all things. The love of God that never fails.[3]

Why would Paul's central theme in 1 Corinthians be love? Because the Christians in Corinth couldn't get along. Driven by self-interest, they were arrogant, rude, and divisive. "You're acting like a bunch of babies," Paul writes harshly. "What you need," he tells them, "is a good dose of the Cross. I don't want to hear about your hostility and sin. Only one thing matters: Jesus Christ and him crucified."[4]

Maybe we could hear Paul saying something like this: "Jesus died so you can live. Now it's time for you to die. To die to yourself, because when you crucify your selfishness, it releases life to others. When you don't, it seems like the problems you have with one another are never resolved. Dying to yourself is good. At first, it hurts like hell (yes, I said that, and I mean it literally). But when you give it up, it lets the peace of God flow into your soul, allowing you to show genuine love for the people you have every reason to hate."

Paul said it this way in his second letter to the Corinthians: "We always carry around in our body the death of Jesus, so that the life of Jesus may also be revealed in our body. For we who are alive are always being given over to death for Jesus' sake, so that his life may be revealed in our mortal body. *So then, death is at work in us, but life is at work in you"* (2 Corinthians 4:10–12, emphasis mine).

Here's an improbable example of how this works. (You're going to wonder if the story you are about to read is true. I'm *not* making this up.) One dark night a dark-hearted man assaulted a forty-something female. A fine, godly woman, she and her husband were looking forward to the second season of their life together. Kids gone, an early retirement not far off, they had nothing ahead of them but their good future. Until that night, when she became pregnant with a child neither of them could ever imagine wanting.

Of course, every woman has the power to give life or end it. In this case, *remarkably,* this middle-aged couple chose to give their child life, a decision complicated by the ethnicity of the rapist. The child would not look much like its mother—and not at all like its father. In order to give life, they had to give theirs: their hopes, their dreams, even their reputations, as so many of their family and friends and everyone they'd meet would forever wonder about their unusual child.

> The desires of self-indulgence are always in opposition to the Spirit, and the desires of the Spirit are in opposition to self-indulgence.
> —Galatians 5:17
> New Jerusalem Bible

The story is absolutely true, as these people have openly shared their pain and joy with the thousands of generous supporters of the Crisis Pregnancy Centers of Greater Phoenix. Once this book is published, I suppose I will be viewed as somewhat of an expert on the way of the Cross; but frankly, I can't imagine what my wife and I would have done if that dark night had been ours. Or how I would feel if my daughter became pregnant that way?

Few of us would carry our cross that far. Maybe someone like Mother Teresa would. You know, there are always those kinds of people around us who make gargantuan sacrifices, and at the very least, we know that our lives should lean that way. Something deep inside each of us says reluctantly, "Yeah . . . there is probably no higher virtue than giving birth to a child of rape." Yes, it seems like, if Jesus had been a woman, he would have done something like that.

It's scandalous.

CROSS-FOLLOWERS ARE MORONIC

Back to 1 Corinthians. The message of the Cross, Paul says, is the entry point, the doorway into a deeper life, a life of true freedom, a life that's lived not for itself but for others. What Paul is teaching, though, isn't easily attained; in fact, it's a way of life so confounding to popular thinking that it's "foolishness to those who are perishing." That is, it makes no sense: When you hear people talk about taking up your cross, it doesn't sound like a door prize, it sounds more like a doormat. I mean, the world just has to laugh at anyone who would give life to a child of rape.

But Paul presses on: "We preach Christ crucified: a stumbling block [*skandalon*, i.e., scandalous] to Jews and foolishness [*moria*, i.e., moronic] to Gentiles." To those whom God has called, though, "both Jews and Greeks, Christ [is] the power of God and the wisdom of God." In other words, what the world considers a sign of weakness is God's power point, and what the world considers foolishness is God's wise way of living: "The foolishness [sacrifice, self-denial] of God is wiser than man's wisdom, and the weakness of God [God embracing death] is stronger than man's strength."[5]

The cross is a scandal of cosmic proportions. It's a scandal to the Gentiles . . . whose world systems are incompatible with Christ's teachings on love, acceptance, forgiveness, humility, meekness. Jesus warns us,

> [Don't be like those people, because] the kings of the
> Gentiles lord it over them. . . . Instead, the greatest among
> you should be like the youngest, and the one who rules like
> the one who serves. For who is greater, the one who is at the
> table or the one who serves? Is it not the one who is at the
> table? But I am among you as one who serves.
>
> LUKE 22:25–27

Scandalous.
The Cross was a scandal to the Jewish community at the time of Christ, too, many of them "fine religious people" who heard Jesus telling them they were not nearly as righteous as they thought. The Cross exposes the limitations of religious self-effort. It's a scandal to my reli-

gion. As we've seen, the once-religious Paul wrote,

> I consider everything [his former very religious life] a loss
> compared to the surpassing greatness of knowing Christ Jesus
> my Lord, for whose sake I have lost all things. I consider
> them rubbish, that I may gain Christ.
>
> PHILIPPIANS 3:8

Remember, *rubbish* is a nice English word for a nasty Greek term that means, literally, "dog droppings."

THE CROSS IS . . .

A scandal to selfish ambition: "Do nothing out of selfish ambition or vain conceit, but in humility consider others better than yourselves."[6] *It's a scandal to self-interest:* "Each of you should look not only to your own interests, but also to the interests of others."[7] *It's a scandal to your reputation:* "Your attitude should be the same as that of Christ Jesus: Who, being in very nature God, did not consider equality with God something to be grasped, but made himself nothing, taking the very nature of a servant, being made in human likeness."[8]

A scandal to human government and business management: "Tell ye the daughter of Zion, Behold, thy King cometh unto thee, meek, and sitting upon an ass, and a colt the foal of an ass."[10] This, of course, is a prophecy about Palm Sunday.

> In any conflict, the first one to the Cross wins.
> —Al Ells[9]

A scandal to husbands: Love your wives as much as Christ loved the church. Be uncharacteristically tender. "Be considerate as you live with your wives, and treat them with respect as the weaker partner and as heirs with you of the gracious gift of life, so that nothing will hinder your prayers."[11]

A scandal to wives: "As the church submits to Christ, so also wives should submit to their husbands in everything."[12]

A scandal to 'tweens and teens: Honor and obey your parents.[13]

A scandal to parents: "Fathers, do not exasperate your children; instead, bring them up in the training and instruction of the Lord."[14]

A scandal to employers: "Provide your [employees] with what is right and fair, because you know that you also have a Master in heaven."[15]

A scandal to employees: Don't work for promotions or pay, work for God. "Obey your earthly masters in everything; and do it, not only when their eye is on you and to win their favor, but with sincerity of heart and reverence for the Lord. Whatever you do, work at it with all your heart, as working for the Lord, not for men, since you know that you will receive an inheritance from the Lord as a reward. It is the Lord Christ you are serving."[16]

A scandal to your personal rights: Give them up. It's scandalous to respond to injustice with patience and love. It's scandalous to decide, once and for all, that you'll never, ever whine, *"That not fair!"* Listen to this:

> What counts is that you put up with it for God's sake when you're treated badly *for no good reason.* There's no particular virtue in accepting punishment that you well deserve. But if you're treated badly for good behavior and continue in spite of it to be a good servant, that is what counts with God.
>
> This is *the kind of life you've been invited into, the kind of life Christ lived.* He suffered everything that came his way so you would know that it could be done, and also know how to do it, step by step.
>
> He never did one thing wrong,
> Not once said anything amiss.
>
> They called him every name in the book and he said nothing back. He suffered in silence, content to let God set things right.

1 PETER 2:19–23 THE MESSAGE, EMPHASIS MINE

A scandal to your pride: Up is down and down is up. "Humble yourselves before the Lord, and he will lift you up."[17]

A scandal to your sensibilities: "Love your enemies and pray for those who persecute you. . . . If you love those who love you, what reward will you get? Are not even the tax collectors doing that? And if you greet only your brothers, what are you doing more than others? Do not even pagans do that? . . ."

"Love your enemies . . . and lend to them without expecting to get anything back. . . .

Do not judge, and you will not be judged. Do not condemn, and you will not be condemned.[18]

Forgive, and you will be forgiven. Give, and it will be given to you."[19]

Make peace with your adversary quickly. Don't go to court over civil matters.[20]

> I have learned that God is not the enemy of my enemies. God is not even the enemy of God's own enemies.
> —Martin Niemoeller

A scandal to your sexuality. Sex is only for marriage: "Marriage should be honored by all, and the marriage bed kept pure, for God will judge the adulterer and all the sexually immoral."[21]

Scandalous.

LOVING THIEVES

And then there is, perhaps, the biggest *skandalon* of all: money. A ministry friend of mine summed up life: "There are only two things in the world: God and money." Certainly, money in and of itself isn't evil, as we remind ourselves,[22] but let's not underestimate its power to control us. Remember, Jesus made it as clear as a window without glass:

> No servant can serve two masters. Either he will hate the one and love the other, or he will be devoted to the one and despise the other. You cannot serve both God and Money.

And then this, and I love it: "The Pharisees, who loved money, heard all this and were sneering at Jesus."[23]

Don't you just love money? C'mon, now. You don't? Then why

does it just make you want to scream when people ask you to give it away? Don't you just hate to be pressured about giving? *And you don't love money?* Stop living in denial! *All of us love money.* Still disagree? What if someone steals your money? Or your favorite things? That doesn't bother you at all? Listen to what Jesus said: "If someone takes your cloak, do not stop him from taking your tunic. Give to everyone who asks you, and if anyone takes what belongs to you, do not demand it back."[24]

Scandalous.

Well, he did say those things, but they don't apply to us today, *right?* I mean, what's he really teaching us? That I shouldn't even lock my house at night? No, there are *many* biblical exhortations (basically) to use our heads, but when Jesus suggests we should happily give the thief whatever he wants, he's exposing the deeply rooted fears, the godlessness, the essential depravity of the human soul. For us, our stuff is often the bottom line. Not faith. Not God. We don't really love our enemies, and at times we can barely love the people we love.

Scandalous!

FROM OUTRAGE TO REVULSION

All of these outrageous biblical commands are entry points into Christ, into the abundant, extreme, eternal life of God we've examined. The Cross happened. It was a historical event. Among other things, the Cross is a symbol of ultimate sacrifice and, for the purpose of this chapter, *revulsion*. What people felt when they first viewed *The Passion of the Christ*—distraught, overwhelmed with sorrow and grief, literally sick to their stomachs, compelled to close their eyes and not watch[25]—all of these reactions speak to us about how the *message* of the Cross makes us feel as well. Watching the crucifixion makes us sick. And, quite frankly, doing what Jesus teaches about life makes us sick. We gnash our teeth in bitter resistance to the scandal that the Cross represents.

Die to yourself.
I scream, *NO!*
Jesus whispers softly, *yes.*

Love your enemies.
I scream, *NO!*
Jesus whispers softly, *yes.*
Forgive the unforgivable.
I scream, *NO!*
Jesus whispers softly, *yes.*
Give away your money and possessions.
I scream, *NO!*
Jesus whispers softly, *yes.*
Wealth and success aren't important.
I scream, *YES THEY ARE!*
Jesus whispers softly, *no they're not.*

This is the scandal of extreme life—radically, wildly different from everything we think we know. Like Neo in *The Matrix* waking up to the real world. Don't you just love the look on his face as he tries to understand a life he's never known? Pain. Atrophy. Hyperventilation. Confusion. Suffocation. Fear.

Neo was *scandalized.*

HOME IMPROVEMENT

I love words. I write. I speak. And I love the ways words work together, like oxymorons, where two words with very different meanings are used to create a unique idea that can only be expressed by the use of those two words together. We've all laughed over such expressions, like "crash landing" . . . or "military intelligence" . . . or "postal worker."

Neo: No. I don't believe it. It's not possible.
Morpheus: I didn't say it would be easy, Neo. I just said it would be the truth.
Neo: Stop. Let me out. Let me out. I want out.

But how about these! I just discovered a great new book by Marty Grothe, *Oxymoronica: Paradoxical Wit & Wisdom From History's Greatest Wordsmiths.* Here are some samples from his Web site:

Writing is easy; all you do is sit staring at a blank sheet of paper until the drops of blood form on your forehead.
—Gene Fowler

A writer is somebody for whom writing is more difficult than it is for other people.
—Thomas Mann

We are all failures—at least, all the best of us are.
—J. M. Barrie

Be obscure clearly.
—E. B. White[26]

While I have you thinking, how about these two words: *broken up*. How about if we arrange the words this way:

UP

BROKEN

As opposed to:

BROKEN

DOWN

Get it? I'm being obscure clearly! Broken up . . . broken down . . . Broken up . . . broken down . . . Make you dizzy?

In other words, when life is difficult, which way is it going to take you? Up or down? Which way are you going to go? Backward or forward? Are you going to take the low road or the high way? Are you going to break down? Or are you going to be broken up?

One of the significant themes in the Bible is *brokenness,* a word that doesn't exist in *either* my factory-fresh Microsoft Word, recently installed on my new laptop, or in WordPerfect 11. I've had to "add to dictionary" in both programs, which to me is a metaphor of how clueless our world is about this essential biblical virtue.

What is brokenness? In his book *Broken in the Right Place,* my friend and fellow pastor Alan Nelson writes, "Brokenness is becoming less so Christ can become more."[27] And Jimmy Seibert says that "brokenness is being completely submitted to God's will." Essentially, brokenness is another way to understand the message of the Cross. Taking up your cross, dying to yourself, is brokenness.

How do you get brokenness? First, you get born. Brokenness is a gift that comes with the initial moment of life, which is why all of us scream in protest at that first gulp of fresh air. Because we live in a fallen world, brokenness is not an option; it *is* going to happen one way or the other. Being obscure clearly, Jesus said of himself, "He who falls on this stone will be broken to pieces, but he on whom it falls will be crushed."[28] In other words, we can choose to be broken, we can choose to take up our cross, or we let life do it for us. Brokenness is being completely submitted to God's will.

PEACHES

Brokenness seems so . . . well . . . bad. How could something that seems so bad actually be so good? Jesus said it this way: "Unless a kernel of wheat falls to the ground and dies, it remains only a single seed. But if it dies, it produces many seeds."[29] Every seed—let's take a peach seed, for example—has life inside a hard shell, and before the life sealed inside can be released, that shell has to be *broken.* Jesus says we have to die to live.

James alludes to this when he writes,

> Is your life full of difficulties and temptations? Then be
> happy, for when the way is rough, your patience has a chance
> to grow. So let it grow, and don't try to squirm out of your
> problems. For when your patience is finally in full bloom,
> then you will be ready for anything, strong in character, full
> and complete.
>
> JAMES 1:2–4 TLB

Still wondering why this is good? It may be good for a peach seed, you say, but not for me. That's the point: dying to self is never, strictly speaking, good for you, because it's not about you. Dying to self is good for everyone else in your life. Turn it around for a moment: If the more difficult people in your life die to self, isn't that wonderful for you?

If your blockheaded friend came to you and said, "I'm really sorry. Your friendship is worth more to me than being right," wouldn't that just make you smile? Wouldn't that make you feel valued, loved, respected? He would be, in that moment, taking up his cross, and his "death" would mean life to you. Think about how powerfully life-giving *you* can be, if you follow Jesus and take up *your* cross.

JARS FOR THE PEACHES

This is why so many places in the Bible present the upside of being broken down. Paul explained it this way:

> We have this treasure in jars of clay to show that this all-surpassing power is from God and not from us. We are hard pressed on every side, but not crushed; perplexed, but not in despair; persecuted, but not abandoned; struck down, but not destroyed. We always carry around in our body the death of Jesus, so that the life of Jesus may also be revealed in our body. For we who are alive are always being given over to death for Jesus' sake, so that his life may be revealed in our mortal body. So then, death is at work in us, but life is at work in you.
>
> 2 CORINTHIANS 4:7–12

> Blessed are the meek, for they will inherit the earth.
> —Jesus

In other words, my loss is your gain, but if I win, you lose. Yeah, you might say, "This situation is killin' me." Hey, maybe that isn't so bad! Brokenness is not only becoming less so Christ can become more, but it's about becoming less so *you* can become more.

What do you want to see in me, Gary Kinnaman, author of this book? Wisdom? Knowledge? Insight? Humor? I had all that when I was preaching a few weeks ago, and then someone interrupted the service by walking up and down the aisle. I stopped being wise and knowledgeable and insightful and funny . . . and told the guy to please sit down. I was ever so slightly irritable.

By that afternoon I had a message on my office voicemail. I don't know how they found my direct number, but they called to tell me that I could have handled the situation better. Two things: First, I can *always* handle *every* situation better. (What else is new?!) Second, all the people in my church who hear me speak every week care much more about my brokenness than they do about my good preaching, because if I give them the slightest indication during a message that I'm irritated, or distracted, or unkind, it swirls all my good teaching right down the baptismal drain.

Here's the lesson: Your family and friends want to see the same thing in you that you want to see in me. And do you know what that "thing" is? *God. Jesus. The Holy Spirit.* People don't care about how right you are, but they do care about how full of God you are. They care about the *peaches,* Christ in you, not the peach *jar.*

> Brokenness and freedom go together, in that order;
> first suffering, then comfort;
> first trouble, then joy;
> first felt unworthiness, then felt love;
> first death to the self, then resurrection of the soul.
> —Larry Crabb, *The Pressure's Off*

> There is no one more beautiful than one who is broken!
> Stubbornness and self-love give way to beauty in one who has been broken by God.
> —Watchman Nee, *The Release of the Spirit*

REMODELING

Here are two transformational life-principles you can speak aloud to God in your private prayer: *First,* tell yourself, *I will let life's conflicts and difficulties have their full God-opportunity effect.* Why is this necessary? Because this old house needs remodeling. When people come to God, *he* never gets a new house.

Have you ever done any remodeling? Lord have mercy! My wife and I majorly remodeled seven rooms in our home. Not one at a time, but all at once, including our master bedroom, master bath, kitchen, and family room. It was a nightmare.

In a support-group meeting with some of my friends, I confessed I was tipping away from God, and my marriage was tipping over. Not that our thirty years together was really in trouble, but I can't ever remember being so stressed about every little thing. Every weekend, of course, I was speeding to the house of God to basically tell everyone in my church how to stay on top of life, how to trust God in everything. As I was encouraging them to break *up,* I was breaking *down.*

One of my friends asked me, "So what do you think God is saying to you?" My entirely unspiritual response was, "I have no idea, and I don't care. I just want to finish the freakin' remodel."

New construction is messy, but you don't have to *live* in the mess! Remodeling is tearing down and tearing up what's already there while you're there right in the middle of it. You have to live and eat and sleep while hammers are pounding and the dust is flying. Our son Matt, when he came home from school one day, stood there staring at the side of our house where I had demolished part of the block wall with a sledge hammer. He laughed, "Wow, it looks like that bombed-out, blown-up town in *Private Ryan.*"

Was it worth it? *Absolutely!* Marilyn and I have enlarged, modernized, and beautified our thirty-year-old home. And we love it . . . but nothing of value in life comes without sacrifice.

THE ROAD LESS TRAVELED

Second, tell yourself, *I will choose the road less traveled. I will embrace the attitude of Christ. I will take the high way of the Cross.*
From an anonymous author on the Web:

> WHEN to do the will of God means that even my Christian brothers will not understand, and I remember that "Neither did His brothers believe in Him" (John 7:5), and I bow my head to obey and accept the misunderstanding, *this is brokenness.*

> WHEN I am misrepresented or deliberately misinterpreted, and I remember that Jesus was falsely accused but He "held His peace," and I bow my head to accept the accusation without trying to justify myself, *this is brokenness.*

> WHEN another is preferred before me and I am deliberately passed over, and I remember that they cried, "Away with this man, and release unto us Barabbas" (Luke 23:18), and I bow my head

and accept rejection, *this is brokenness.*

WHEN my plans are brushed aside, and I see the work of years brought to ruins by the ambitions of others, and I remember that Jesus allowed them to lead Him away to crucify Him (Matt. 27:31), and He accepted that place of failure, and I bow my head and accept the injustice without bitterness, *this is brokenness.*

WHEN in order to be right with my God it is necessary to take the humbling path of confession and restitution, and I remember that Jesus "made Himself of no reputation" and "humbled Himself . . . unto death, even the death of the cross" (Phil. 2:8), and I bow my head and am ready to accept the shame of exposure, *this is brokenness.*

WHEN others take unfair advantage of my being a Christian and treat my belongings as public property, and I remember "they stripped Him . . . and parted His garments, casting lots" (Matt. 27:28, 35), and I bow my head and accept "joyfully the spoiling of my goods" for His sake, *this is brokenness.*

WHEN one acts toward me in an unforgivable way, and I remember that when He was crucified Jesus prayed, "Father, forgive them; for they know not what they do" (Luke 23:34), and I bow my head and accept any behavior toward me as permitted by my loving Father, *this is brokenness.*

WHEN people expect the impossible of me and more than time or human strength can give, and I remember that Jesus said, "This is My body which is given for you" (Luke 22:19), and I repent of my self-indulgence and lack of self-giving for others, *this is brokenness.*[30]

THE SCANDAL OF THE LITTLE WAY

Perhaps no one understood the way of the Cross better than Thérèse of Lisieux. Master of spiritual formation Richard Foster writes,

This simple woman, known only as "the Little Flower," devised a prayer-filled approach to life that has helped many. This

Little Way, as she called it, is deceptively simple. It is, in short, to seek out the menial job, to welcome unjust criticisms, to befriend those who annoy us, to help those who are ungrateful. For her part, Thérèse was convinced that these "trifles" please Jesus more than the great deeds of recognized holiness. The beauty of the Little Way is how it is utterly available to everyone. . . . Almost daily we can give smiling service to nagging co-workers, listen attentively to silly bores, express little kindnesses without making a fuss.

We may think these tiny, trivial activities are hardly worth mentioning. That, of course, is precisely their value. They are unrecognized conquests over selfishness. We will never receive a medal or even a "thank-you" for these invisible victories in ordinary life—which is exactly what we want.

An incident from Thérèse's autobiography, *The Story of a Soul,* underscores the hiddenness of the Little Way. One uneducated and rather conceited sister had managed to irritate Thérèse in everything she did. Rather than avoid the person, however, she [Thérèse] took the Little Way straight into the conflict. "I set myself to treat her as if I loved her best of all." Thérèse succeeded so well in her Little Way that following her death this same sister declared, "During her life, I made her really happy."[31]

FOR REFLECTION AND DISCUSSION

Over a period of a week or so, make a list (yes, write them down) of the things that happen in your life that upset you, the things that cause some measure of distress, even outrage. Then give some thought to each of those moments. Ask yourself: Why is this something that troubles me? What do I need to give up? What does it mean for me to take up my cross? Remember, when scandalous, outrageous things happen to you, it always seems *more* scandalous, *more* outrageous, to respond the way Jesus would.

How do you define freedom for yourself? What, specifically, are some things you are doing to live in that freedom? In what ways are you giving up, letting go? What's difficult for you to give up, to let go? Why? How can you invite Jesus into that?

CHAPTER THIRTEEN

The Scandal of Forgiveness

God of forgiveness, do not forgive those who committed these crimes.
   —Elie Wiesel

Father, forgive them, for they do not know what they are doing.
   —Jesus

It was bitter cold.

The leafless trees stood like headless human skeletons. Their branches, so many fleshless arms and hands, were frozen skyward over the distant villages of brown-brick homes. Patches of crusty snow littered the silent, frozen fields. I was wearing a long coat over a jacket over a sweater, and I still felt the chill.

It was late winter in Poland, and my friends and I were walking somberly toward the castle-like entrance to the most infamous of all Nazi extermination camps. *Auschwitz.*[1] Bundled in our bulky winter garments, we shuffled down the rusty railroad tracks, through the massive gates, and into a vast wasteland of concrete slabs, the foundations of long wooden buildings where hundreds of thousands of people had lived and loved . . . and died.

On the horizon of the death camp were the remains of the ovens. Lonely, blackened chimneys silhouetted against the cold lead-gray sky.

We were alone.

And silent.

With the faceless, voiceless ghosts of a million souls.

A few years later an Associated Press photo of the same ominous gate appeared on the front page of the Phoenix newspaper. Alongside it was an article about the fiftieth anniversary of the liberation of Auschwitz, and the reporter began by quoting the prayer of prominent Nazi-hunter Elie Wiesel: "God of forgiveness, do not forgive those who committed these crimes." For a glimpse of why someone would pray so bitterly, consider this journal entry of Wiesel's life:

> Never shall I forget that night, the first night in camp, which has turned my life into one long night, seven times cursed and seven times sealed. Never shall I forget that smoke. Never shall I forget the little faces of the children, whose bodies I saw turned into wreaths of smoke beneath a silent blue sky.
>
> Never shall I forget those flames which consumed my faith forever. Never shall I forget that nocturnal silence which deprived me, for all eternity, of the desire to live. Never shall I forget those moments which murdered my God and my soul and turned my dreams to dust. Never shall I forget these things, even if I am condemned to live as long as God Himself. Never.[2]

Do you feel the same way? Are there some things God absolutely won't forgive? Can't forgive? Are there some things *you* won't or can't forgive? Is "unforgivable" a word in your vocabulary? Or is it more than a word, like a dark creature in the basement of your soul?

"THE SIN OF FORGIVENESS"

In *Shoah,* Claude Lanzmann's documentary on the holocaust, a leader of the Warsaw Ghetto uprising talked about the bitterness that fifty years later remains in his soul over how he and his neighbors were treated by the Nazis. "If you could lick my heart," he sneered, "it would poison you."

Some people think extreme forgiveness is a sin. That's the title of a Dennis Prager article that appeared a few years ago in the *Wall Street Journal:*

> The bodies of the three teenage girls murdered by a fellow student at Heath High School . . . were not yet cold before the students of the Christian prayer group that was shot at announced, "We forgive you, Mike." . . .
>
> Over the past generation, the idea that a central message of Christianity is to forgive everyone who commits evil against anyone, no matter how great and cruel and whether or not the evildoer ever repents, has been adopted by much of Christendom. . . . This doctrine undermines the moral foundations of American civilization because it advances the amoral notion that no matter how much you hurt other people, millions of your fellow citizens will immediately forgive you.[3]

And just a few miles down the street from my church, Jeffrie G. Murphy, Affiliated Professor of Religious Studies at Arizona State University, has written a book about forgiveness with a delicious title: *Getting Even: Forgiveness and Its Limits:*

> Vindictive emotions (anger, resentment, and a desire for revenge) actually deserve a more legitimate place in our emotional, social, and legal lives than we currently recognize, while forgiveness [part of what the book calls a staple of "current pop psychology dogma"]—though often a great virtue—deserves to be more selectively granted.[4]

GOOD ANGER

Certainly it's not healthy simply to suppress our emotions. I even encourage people to find a friend with whom they can share openly their deepest and most "sinful" feelings. After all, the Bible instructs us to confess our sins "to each other and pray for each other so that you may be healed," for "the prayer of a righteous man is powerful and effective."[5]

The Bible itself refuses to shy away from the reality of human pain and how it makes us feel about others. The writers of the Psalms, for example, express freely the full range of emotions, from ecstatic joy to hostile despair. In one place the psalmist curses his enemy:

> May his children be fatherless and his wife a widow. May his children be wandering beggars; may they be driven from their ruined homes. May a creditor seize all he has; may strangers plunder the fruits of his labor. May no one extend kindness to him or take pity on his fatherless children. May his descendants be cut off, their names blotted out from the next generation.
>
> PSALM 109:9–13

Nasty.

Again, though, the New Testament edges us away from unbridled anger: "Do not let the sun go down while you are still angry,"[6] Paul wrote to the Ephesians, and to the Romans he insisted,

> Do not take revenge, my friends, but leave room for God's wrath, for it is written: "It is mine to avenge; I will repay," says the Lord.
>
> On the contrary: "If your enemy is hungry, feed him; if he is thirsty, give him something to drink. In doing this, you will heap burning coals on his head." Do not be overcome by evil, but overcome evil with good.
>
> ROMANS 12:19–21

Why? Because as necessary as it may be for us to feel fully our feelings, we dare not let our feelings become lord of our soul, as the writer of Hebrews warns: "See to it that no one misses the grace of God and that no bitter root grows up to cause trouble and defile many."[7] Bitterness—and unforgiveness, oxygen in the fire of hostility—is not just about a pity party in the privacy of your own heart and mind; according to very recent research by the Institute of Forgiveness,[8] it's viciously, cancerously destructive to your thoughts, your emotions, even your health. And it has the potential to do terrible things to the people around you.

Is there hope? Or are there things outside the limits of forgiveness? Are there things that should *never* be forgiven? How deeply have you been hurt? Do you feel trapped by the pain? Enslaved by the hatred and fury you feel toward "that person"? Your father? Your mother? The people at your last job? Maybe you lost your job because of *those* people.

MORE SLAVERY

Are you a slave of the ones who hurt you? Like Joseph, the guy in the Bible who annoyed his brothers so much they sold him to slave traders?[9] Facing dire straits, however, *those* brothers later found themselves at a reunion.

Joseph recognized them, but he was older, and his brothers hadn't seen him for years. He was dressed Egyptian-style, too, and he spoke through an interpreter until finally he beckoned, "'Come close to me.' When they had done so,

> Whoever fights monsters should see to it that in the process he does not become a monster. And if you gaze long enough into an abyss, the abyss will gaze back into you.
> —Friedrich Nietzsche

he said, 'I am your brother Joseph, the one you sold into Egypt!'" Can you picture their faces? Can you hear them gasp? Can you imagine their terror of his retribution? But instead, Joseph said,

> Do not be distressed and do not be angry with yourselves for selling me here, because it was to save lives that God sent me ahead of you. For two years now there has been famine in the land, and for the next five years there will not be plowing and reaping. But God sent me ahead of you to preserve for you a remnant on earth and to save your lives by a great deliverance. So then, *it was not you who sent me here, but God.*
> GENESIS 45:4–8, EMPHASIS MINE

Joseph was either out of his mind or on to something. Under the circumstances, any other *normal* person would have had his brothers hung. At the very least, he would have put them in prison and kept them there for a long time. Maybe as long as they'd kept him from his beloved father.

Yes, after all those years in a foreign land, after all those years away from my home, I would have wanted to get in a few licks of vengeance. It makes me feel indignant just to sit here and write about Joseph . . . and about kids in my church who've been murdered . . . and about the holocaust. How can those kinds of things, those kinds of people, be forgiven?

Forgiveness is a scandal of divine proportions.

Was it a sin for Joseph to forgive his brothers? Or does this ancient narrative tell us something about the amazing possibilities of giving ourselves entirely to God? When Joseph saw his family, he didn't just keep his cool; he kept his perspective. He kept telling himself that, through it all, God was in control. That God, somehow, brings life out of death.

BRAGGING ABOUT INCEST

I'd like to offer some thoughts on the nature, necessity, and effects of the scandal of forgiveness from a somewhat unfamiliar Bible text, 2 Corinthians 2:5–11. The background for this passage is pretty twisted. From Paul's first letter to the Corinthians, we know that a member of the church was committing incest—and flaunting it. Not surprisingly, his behavior was putting a black mark on the whole church.[10]

When we read Paul's second letter to the Corinthians, however, we hear that the church there had taken responsibility for the problem and had confronted the sinner. Let's look at what Paul says about contrition and forgiveness.

First we learn that *there's no such thing as a personal offense.* Even though every pain in life feels personal (I get personally upset with the hammer if I hit my thumb, and I've been heard shouting at my computer), it's not just about you and your personal pain:

> *If anyone has caused grief, he has not so much grieved me as he has grieved all of you, to some extent—not to put it too severely.*

In other words, Paul is telling us, as offended as he was about the

Corinthian problem, he didn't take the offense personally.

Whatever somebody does to hurt somebody else always ends up hurting lots of other people, like the children, the relatives and friends of the one hurt. Even if the hurt is too personal to talk about with anybody, even if the hurt is a family secret, it still has a ripple effect, because any emotional damage in you or me will always, in some way, affect how we love or don't love others.

Years ago I met with a beautiful young couple whose parents were leaders in our church. They'd asked me to do their wedding, and during the second premarital session, the young man let me know he hated his mother. Well, he didn't actually *say* he hated his mother—he told me calmly, with a pleasant smile on his face, that he was not inviting her or his father to the wedding. I gasped, "You're not inviting your parents to the wedding? Your dad is an elder in the church!"

He smiled again as he told me he didn't want his mother to have anything to do with his life. Ever. And his bride-to-be passionately agreed, because she had formed her own perceptions of what her mother-in-law-to-be was like.

Stunned, I told them firmly, "If you don't invite your parents to the wedding, then I don't do the wedding."

A few weeks later they were back in my office. "So did you communicate with your parents?"

"No," he smiled.

Turning to the young woman, I predicted, "If your fiancé doesn't deal with his hostility toward his mother, no matter how justified he feels, guess what? He's going to turn his anger toward you." (That's known as *transference*.)

Under pressure from Pastor Gary—me—they relented and invited his parents, but he absolutely refused to deal with his deeper issues. Just six months into their marriage, my phone rang. It was the young wife. She spoke very quietly. Like she didn't want to be overheard. Her voice quivering, she whispered, "My husband just beat me up."

I told her, "You have to leave immediately."

I don't think she ever saw him again. He probably just grinned and said, "That's okay."

Forgiveness isn't just about you: It's about what the offense does to everyone you know, how it transfers to everyone you know—including your closest friends, the ones who lick your poisoned heart. The starting point for understanding the need to forgive is outside yourself. Look around. How are the hot coals of unforgiveness in your own heart burning the souls of people you love? How is your bitterness leaking into their lives?

LET YOUR PROBLEM BE GOD'S PROBLEM

Second, just as there's no such thing as a strictly personal offense, *there are multiple consequences for the offender.* Paul writes, "The punishment inflicted on him by the majority is sufficient for him."

In other words, what goes around comes around. To me this is a reminder that vengeance truly is something that belongs to God. His justice—in this life, in the next generation, or in the life to come—is certain. Jesus said,

> Things that cause people to sin are bound to come, but woe to that person through whom they come. It would be better for him to be thrown into the sea with a millstone tied around his neck than for him to cause one of these little ones to sin. So watch yourselves.
>
> LUKE 17:1–3

The process of forgiving others *and* my personal healing begin when I refuse to take things personally. The next step is to remind myself that, ultimately, God is the one who will address the problem. And if he doesn't? If God seems to do nothing? Then his grace will be sufficient to sustain me in the presence of injustice.[11] I must learn from Jesus on his way to the cross: "When they hurled their insults at him, he did not retaliate; when he suffered, he made no threats." And I love this part: "Instead, he entrusted himself to him who judges justly."[12]

Can you do that?

Can Jesus do that in you? How big is your problem? How big is your Jesus? After all, isn't Jesus the embodiment of divine forgiveness?

Third, forgiveness releases God's love. Getting back to our main passage, Paul writes to the Corinthians,

> Now instead, you ought to forgive and comfort him, so that he will not be overwhelmed by excessive sorrow. I urge you, therefore, to reaffirm your love for him.

Forgiveness is a release, a letting go. It has the potential to change the person we forgive, if she receives it, but if she doesn't, it still has the power to change us. On the other hand, unforgiveness keeps the hurt and pain alive. In fact, unforgiveness *empowers* the hurt and pain.

> Unforgiveness keeps *raising* the issue.
> Forgiveness keeps *razing* the issue.

The Chronicle of Higher Education, a newspaper for college and university professors, did a major article on what they call "the field of forgiveness studies." How about this for a hook? The article states, "Despite high hopes, researchers have not demonstrated that conflict-management skills help keep married couples together." Instead, UCLA professor of psychology Thomas Bradbury urges two things: *forgiveness and empathy.*[13]

Sociologists and counselors are rediscovering an ancient virtue and a primal power: forgiveness. William Damon, Professor of Education at Stanford University, admits, "There's a whole bunch of stuff which religious people talk about all the time that social scientists never talk about, or tend to reduce to the trivial."[14]

> You always become the thing you fight most. It is a fact that cannot be denied: The wickedness of others becomes our own wickedness because it kindles something evil in our own hearts.
> —Carl Jung

That's changing, though; according to recent work funded by the Templeton Campaign for Forgiveness Research, there are "'robust' physiological differences between nonforgiving and forgiving states. Subjects' cardiovascular systems labor when they remember the person who hurt them. Gut stress is 'significantly greater' when they consider revenge rather than forgiveness."

The researchers found that "we may be drawn to hold grudges 'because that makes us feel like we are more in control and we are less sad.'" But interviews with the subjects of the project "indicate that they felt in even greater control when they tried to empathize with their offenders and enjoyed the greatest sense of power, well-being and resolution when they managed to grant forgiveness."[15]

Backward thinking! Outrageous! A scandal!

This research, perhaps, answers a couple of tough questions, like, when is the past really past? How can you know you have forgiven the person who has deeply wounded you? The answer: by whether or not the pain of the past is losing its grip on your present. Louis Smedes writes,

> If you cannot free people from their wrongs and see them as the needy people they are, you enslave yourself to your own painful past and by fastening yourself to the past, you let your hate become your future.[16]

A GOOD EXCUSE NOT TO FORGIVE

The other tough question is this: *"But what if the pain-maker isn't repentant?"* In his article on "the sin of forgiveness," which I referenced at the beginning of this chapter, Dennis Prager writes, "The feel-good doctrine of automatic forgiveness . . . destroys Christianity's central moral tenets about forgiveness—that forgiveness, even by God, is contingent on the sinner repenting."

There are, of course, many places in Scripture where forgiveness seems to be conditional. Take the Lord's Prayer for example: "Forgive us our debts, as we also have forgiven our debtors."[17] I agree, I can't forgive another person in such a way that the problem between us simply goes away. God can't even do that. He offers every one of us forgiveness in the finished work of Christ on the cross, but that forgiveness comes to us only when we believe.

Remember that when the criminal on the cross next to Jesus said, "Jesus, remember me," Jesus promised, "Today you will be with me in paradise."[18] To the criminal on the other cross, Jesus said nothing: It was the silence of hell. Even when Jesus said of those who were nailing him to the cross, "Father, forgive them, for they do not know what they are doing,"[19] his prayer didn't send the Roman ghouls straight to heaven.

But he still said it. And meant it. I have to believe that when Christ forgave those who were crucifying him, it did something for him, humanly speaking. No, forgiving others, for Jesus, wasn't some self-stroking psychobabble. For him and for us, *forgiving others releases us from the dead-end of unforgiveness and releases the power of God's sustaining and healing presence into our lives.*

Forgiveness is a phone booth out of the matrix of hate, which is precisely why Jesus taught us to pray, "Release us from our sins, as we release others from theirs."[20] God's power to forgive us releases us to forgive others, but conversely, when we forgive others, it releases the power of God's forgiveness in us.

So does forgiveness condone the sin of the one who causes you pain? Of course not. Should the person who caused you pain repent? Of course. If he repents, will it make it easier for you to forgive him? Yes. Will he repent if you forgive him first, or if you promise to forgive him if he does? Maybe, but probably not. If you're really angry with someone, though, no matter how much he repents or tries to repent, his penance will probably never be enough to make your anger go away. Only you can do that, and you can only do it by taking your pain to the Cross.

> To forgive is not to condone, and it is certainly not to forget.
> —Ron Enroth

TO YOUR HEALTH!

So I go back to this: Forgiveness is (1) always about God first, and (2) always good for you, no matter how the other person responds. Forgiveness is release—for God's sake, for the offender's sake, and for your sake:

- *Psychological benefit:* healing our mind and emotions
- *Physical benefit:* neutralizing our life-threatening anger
- *Relational benefit:* holding out hope for reconciliation
- *Spiritual benefit:* being forgiven as we forgive others

- *Kingdom benefit:* our love and forgiveness attracts others to Christ, because everyone, everywhere is looking for the perfect world where people love and forgive one another perfectly. Of all that Christians have to offer, nothing is more outrageously appealing than unconditional love, acceptance, and forgiveness.

Fourth, forgiveness is an act of obedience. Or, to say it another way, *forgiveness starts with a choice.* Back to our text, Paul says,

> *The reason I wrote you was to see if you would stand the test and be obedient in everything. If you forgive anyone, I also forgive him.*

Jesus didn't die on the cross because he felt like it. No, it was the last thing he *wanted* to do. In the Garden of Gethsemane, "being in anguish, he prayed more earnestly, and his sweat was like drops of blood falling to the ground."[21] As he kept praying, though, he found peace in accepting God's will: "My Father, if it is not possible for this cup to be taken away unless I drink it, may your will be done."[22] Jesus didn't run to the cross—he staggered there, and died.

Forgiveness is impossible without suffering, pain, and sacrifice— the suffering brought on by those who cause us pain, and the sacrifice of personal restraint, the decision to love and forgive them. Maybe the decision not to kill them!

Instead, it feels like what they've done is killing us. When my emotions scream, *Vengeance! Give them what they deserve!* the Spirit of God in me says, *Give them Jesus. Give them what they don't deserve. Give them what God gave you, even though you didn't deserve it. Forgive them and give them grace.*

SEVEN TIMES A DAY

It's not just *hard* to forgive. It's likely the most difficult thing any of us ever has to do, and the greater the offense, the more difficult it is to forgive. Bestselling author Philip Yancey wrote,

> Forgiveness is no sweet, platonic ideal to be dispensed to the world like perfume sprayed from a fragrance bottle. It is achingly difficult. Long after you have forgiven, the wound lives on in memory.[23]

In extreme human suffering, forgiveness is humanly impossible. Listen again to Elie Wiesel's prayer: "God of forgiveness, don't forgive." Sigmund Freud agreed: "One must forgive one's enemies, but not before they are hanged." And the poet W. H. Auden wrote,

> I and the public know
> > what all school children learn;
> those to whom evil is done
> > do evil in return.

Forgiveness, as the Bible presents it, both the forgiveness that comes from God to us and the forgiveness God expects in us for others, is an unnatural act, a *skandalon*. Forgiveness takes us to outer limits, above and beyond ordinary human life. The obedient, unreasonable act of forgiveness takes us out of the matrix of our bitterness into the extreme life of God. Forgiveness is a portal to the divine. Forgiveness engages us with the love and grace of the God of the universe. Forgiveness is an entry point into a life of freedom from ourselves and freedom to serve others, especially those who don't deserve it.

> *The Cross is the center of God's universe, and forgiveness in the heart of Christ is the center of the Cross.*

I've decided that choosing to forgive is an act of faith, "the substance of things hoped for, the evidence of things not seen."[24] Because forgiveness is humanly unnatural, it's impossible without faith. It has to be a God-thing or it's no-thing. Jesus confounded his disciples with this:

> If your brother sins, rebuke him, and if he repents, forgive him. If he sins against you seven times in a day, and seven times comes back to you and says, "I repent," forgive him.[25]

Think about that. Really. Like you're going to forgive someone who robs your house seven times *in one day*? Or someone who clicks on a virus-infected email that shuts down the network seven times *in one day*? Or who slaps your mother seven times *in one day*? Or who borrows money from you seven times *in one day*? Or who cuts you off on the freeway . . . the *same* guy in the *same* monster truck . . . seven times *in one day*? Or who insults you seven times *in one day*? As if, by the fifth or sixth time, we're going to just let it go, even if they say they're sorry? I don't think so.

- Accepting and forgiving are different processes. We accept persons for the good that they are or do. We forgive persons for the evil that they did or caused.
- Excusing and forgiving are different processes. We excuse people when we no longer hold them accountable. We forgive people when we hold them accountable but do not excuse.
- Tolerating and forgiving are different processes. We tolerate what another has done when we overlook or ignore. We forgive what we cannot tolerate, will not overlook, or ignore.
- Forgetting and forgiving are different processes. We do not need to forgive if we can simply forget. We do not forget when we forgive, but the meaning of the memory changes.
  —David Augsburger[26]

In a parallel text, Jesus tells Peter, who asks him if forgiving seven times is enough, "I tell you, not seven times, but seventy-seven times."[27]

Get it? Jesus is saying that forgiveness is *totally* a God-thing. It's like going to heaven on your own: you can't. You have to be born again. And forgiving others? You have to go where your own energy and effort will never take you, but you can and must go helplessly and humbly to God. This is why the disciples, after being told to forgive seven times in one day, cried out to Jesus, "*Increase our faith!*"[28] Usually, we've heard that famous statement in the context of what follows, as Jesus teaches them about mustard-seed faith, but, in fact, their appeal for increased faith was a prayer to be able to do the crazy, humanly impossible, unnatural act of repeatedly forgiving someone.

PRAYING DOWN THE WRATH OF GOD

Practically, how do you do that? How do you choose to forgive; how do you obey the Bible when it tells you to forgive, when you are powerless in the presence of your anger and pain? I can tell you what's helped me: prayer *for* the pain-giver. No, this hasn't entirely cured my unforgiveness cancer, but prayer for my enemies has put it into remission. Have you ever prayed judgment prayers? Like, "God, deal with that person. Deal with my boss. Deal with my teenager. Deal with my neighbor." Like God is as angry as we are. Like God is going to strike them dead. Of course, we wouldn't kill them, because we're Christians! But *God* can!

How many of our prayers are nothing more than whining complaints? In the fog of our self-obsession, we so seldom think about God's grander purpose. We just want him to take away the irritation or the pain. You know, people like to say, "I don't need that person in my life." Certainly God must agree, right?

Well, actually, Jesus expects us to do something scandalous. As we've seen, he taught his followers to pray *for* their enemies, not against them: "Bless those who curse you, pray for those who mistreat you."[29] In the Greek text, the term translated "for" is *peri,* as in "*peri*scope," which means "to look *around.*" I suppose we could translate this, "Pray *around* those who mistreat you." Ask God to touch every area of their lives, and be positive. Let your prayers be a source of blessing and peace for you and others, not a kind of white magic, where you suggest to God what he should or shouldn't do with people you don't like.

> We aren't being asked to like the other person, because that would require an emotion that we sometimes can't conjure up. But in effect, we are to treat them as though we like them—because that's a decision of our will. We don't have to approve of what they are, what they've done, or how they conduct their affairs, but we are to love who they are—people who matter to God, just like you and I.
> —Lee Strobel,
> *God's OutrageousClaims*

I know, praying *for* your enemies is another one of those outrageously impossible things to do, but it's one of the best ways to start the process of healing in your soul, because prayer not only releases God's power to love the needy pain-giver, but it releases God's love into your own heart and allows you to see the whole problem more from God's point of view.

Forgiveness is an unnatural, outrageous virtue—yes, to forgive is totally divine. Recently I read this extraordinary story of forgiveness in one of the world's least likely places: Bosnia, where ethnic hatred and cleansing are centuries old.

From the beginning Nikola had decided that the best way to win people to Christ was to live as a Christian and let his life speak for itself. Then if anyone asked why he did what he did, he would feel free to tell them. In an age of endless talk, it was an unusual form of evangelism. . . . It *was* unusual in Nikola's new line of work: overseeing the distribution of aid for the international, all-volunteer relief agency known as Agape. . . .

Whenever a stranger would ask Nikola why he did what he did, he would share the burden on his heart: forgiveness did not come from the outside. Each person had to be changed from the inside, and only God could do that. No one could forgive until he or she had God's peace inside.

> There is no future without forgiveness.
> —Desmond Tutu

"Nikola," I asked him, "reconciliation seems to be the current buzzword in Bosnia. I mean, all sorts of groups and business consultants, even experts on conflict resolution, are coming over here from the States, all excited about helping to rehab Bosnia. What do you think about them?"

He nodded and shot off an answer. . . . "These people set up their workshops and bring young people together for sporting or social or cultural events. They mean well. But the communists did the same sort of thing with no lasting success." . . .

There were people, he explained, who wanted all relief and humanitarian aid distributed by nonreligious organizations such as the Red Cross, but they missed the point. You could feed a starving man and temporarily satisfy his physical hunger, but unless you also satisfied his spiritual hunger, he would only become hungry again and be ready to go back to war. Without forgiveness, there could be no reconciliation . . . and only God could enable forgiveness.

Psychiatrists and psychologists claimed that time was all they needed. Give them enough time, and the deepest wounds would heal. But what happened after World War II put the lie to this. The hard evidence was that the majority of the people hurt by their neighbors *never* forgave them, no matter how much time passed—even forty-three years.

"Let me ask you something," Nikola challenged. "If someone invades your land, kills your children, rapes your wife—what would you need to be able to forgive them?"

I already knew the answer, because I had already asked myself the same question. "A miracle," I murmured.

Nikola said, "Jesus is the *only* one who can heal such wounds. No setting up of partitions, no human effort can make your heart able to forgive."

He stood up. "I am convinced that our personal relationship with God is what matters!" he exclaimed. "If I really have a relationship with Him, He will give me the power to forgive. He will give me the power to love those whom I have every reason in the world to hate."[30]

Much closer to home, a woman in my church wrote to me:

> Somewhere around nine years ago you did a teaching series on the Beatitudes. I remember what the title was of the teaching, "Blessed are the merciful, for they shall be shown mercy." Sorry, I have to admit I remember very little of the teaching itself! When I came into the sanctuary that day, though, the worship was awesome. As I closed my eyes so I could fully embrace the presence of God, I saw a vision of Jesus with his arms extended toward me. I was overcome with amazement.
>
> When I opened my eyes to see what had caused me to see such a thing, nothing was there, and I wondered if anyone else had seen what I had seen. No one else seemed especially excited, and as we sat down together, I looked in the church program and saw what you were talking about. "Blessed are the merciful . . ." I remember wondering to myself, "What are you going to say to me today, Lord?"
>
> The thought of my father kept coming to me. He had been emotionally and physically abusive. A police officer, he often treated us kids like the criminals he regularly arrested. I had no hope that my relationship with him would be healed in my lifetime. After church that Sunday, though, I had a deep feeling that God was asking me to extend mercy to my father, who didn't deserve it. So I prayed . . . and wrote my dad a letter. It was so

hard, because I couldn't really remember very many good things about him. When he received it, he made very little of it, and for a moment I was hurt, but Jesus spoke to me and said that *the letter was never really for my dad. All along it was for me.*

> When someone treats you like dirt, you treat them like gold.
> —Truman Madsen

Extending mercy to my father, though, began a process of forgiveness and healing that now spans nine years. Why am I writing now? Because my father, who is now seventy-two, called me *this week* and asked to take me to lunch. With tears in his eyes he asked *me* to forgive *him*! This is such a miracle, I wanted you to know.

Hey, you. Yes, you. You're reading this book. What little steps toward reconciliation and forgiveness can you begin to take to change your world?

Fifth, just as there is no such thing as a strictly personal offense (see point #1 way back there), *there is no such thing as strictly personal forgiveness.* Remember, I am taking you through a short passage in 2 Corinthians, where Paul is giving instructions about forgiveness and healing:

> If you forgive anyone, I also forgive him. And what I have forgiven—if there was anything to forgive—I have forgiven in the sight of Christ for your sake.

Just as a "root of bitterness" is inside of you poisoning others, forgiveness is never entirely personal. We need each other to forgive, and often we need to forgive *together.* In fact, in view of everything the Bible says about Christian community, I believe that I not only need the power of Christ working in me to forgive the unforgivable, I need others to help me forgive. There's awesome power in a group of people forgiving someone together. Really, nobody sins alone and nobody forgives alone. In fact, many are exploring and rediscovering the transformational energy of entire societies looking beyond past injustices and avoiding cycles of revenge.[31]

Sixth, in the final verse in the passage we have been considering, *unforgiveness is a devil of a problem:*

What I have forgiven—if there was anything to forgive—I have forgiven in the sight of Christ for your sake, *in order that Satan might not outwit us. For we are not unaware of his schemes.*

Jesus suggests the dark spiritual implications of unforgiveness as well in the parable of the unforgiving servant.[32] That bitter man had a fellow servant arrested for owing him a few dollars, right after his own master forgave him a debt of thousands.

So angry was the master that he threw the unforgiving servant into prison to be tortured until his entire debt was paid. Not good, because when you look at the story carefully, you realize the wicked servant owed more than he could pay in decades. It's a life sentence of self-inflicted torment.

If unforgiveness is a devil of a problem, then logically God is the only solution. Be strong in the Lord, because our conflict is not with people, but with principalities and powers of darkness.[33] This, perhaps, is another reason why we find forgiveness so difficult to practice. It's a "life-or-death fight to the finish against the Devil and all his angels."[34]

> Unforgiveness is a weapon of mass destruction.
> Forgiveness releases the restorational, transformational
> power of God.

THE LIMITATIONS OF THIS CHAPTER

It's not possible, of course, to address every issue and answer every question about forgiveness in a single chapter. If what I've written has stirred your heart, and you want to read more about this theme, I strongly urge you to read and pray through two extraordinary books: *The Art of Forgiving: When You Need to Forgive and Don't Know How,* by Lewis Smedes,[35] and *Forgiving and Reconciling: Bridges to Wholeness and Hope,* by Everett L. Worthington.[36] Lewis Smedes has helped me greatly. In the most difficult time of my life, when I was deeply hurt by and angry about a number of former friends, I read his first book, *Forgive and Forget,*[37] over and over. I couldn't read it without crying.

I've written this final chapter for a singular reason:

Forgiveness takes us to the heart of the Cross. Forgiveness is the theological and practical center of the Christian faith. God cannot be known apart from forgiveness, and none of us can enjoy rich relationships with one another without the risk of pain and the consequent practice of forgiveness.

Human love has limits, boundaries. The love of God does not—it's boundless. Where human love ends, God's unconditional love begins. Like the Sermon on the Mount—everything Jesus had to say about what it *really* means to love and serve God—forgiveness takes us to the outer limits of our good efforts to be godly. God is love, and that means wildly more than "I love you." God's love is extreme, and forgiveness in a ghetto of the holocaust is a scandal.

Or at Columbine High School in Littleton, Colorado. At this very moment I'm writing on a plane departing Denver, just two days after the fifth anniversary of the shootings. A public schoolteacher in my church handed me this poem, written by two fifth-grade girls in May 1999:

Lives cut short
Faces sad
Broken hearts of moms and dads
What a waste of life they had
Everyone is asking why
Friends and neighbors left to cry
Seeking answers we must try
Now comes the choice
Hate or forgive
Backward or forward
To take or give
Those left behind still have to live
Forgive and live
Healing to bring
God gives the song that loving hearts sing
But hate, you see, ruins everything
So though you're sad
Your pain is real
Maybe angry is how you feel
Choose to forgive and dare to heal

FOR REFLECTION AND DISCUSSION

Write down four or five statements or thoughts in this chapter that were especially meaningful to you. Then write down *why* those thoughts were special. Share them with someone you love, and let them encounter the reality of Christ-life with you.

Who is the person you have the most difficulty forgiving? (Perhaps there are two or three.) If you're discussing your feelings in a group, it may be best not to mention their name(s). Based on what you've read in this chapter, write down three or four specific steps you are going to take each day to escape from the prison of unforgiveness. Keep this list handy as a daily reminder and prayer guide; you may even want to type it out and laminate it. I don't want you to have merely read and enjoyed this book: I want you to believe *into* God's reality, to encounter Jesus and his transformational power!

May the grace of the Lord Jesus Christ, †
and the love of God, †
and the fellowship of the Holy Spirit †
be with you all. †
Amen. †

Endnotes

CHAPTER ONE *Love Like You Can't Imagine*

1. No, my brother isn't rich—he's a public schoolteacher. He borrowed money against my mother's debt-free home.
2. Philippians 2:8.
3. See 1 John 3:16.
4. See Matthew 16:24.
5. Matthew 6:10 KJV.

CHAPTER TWO *Reality: Looking for a Phone Booth*

1. It's not exactly explained how this works, but phone booths are points of escape from the dark reality of the Matrix.
2. More about bridges in the next chapter.
3. John 14:6, emphasis mine.
4. This Greek term, *hodos,* means "path" or "road."
5. See John 10.
6. See Acts 9.
7. See 1 Corinthians 15:1–8.
8. E.g., see 2 Timothy 4:2–5.
9. I am fully aware of the concerns of so many Bible-believing Christians in this regard, and I fully affirm that God's Word is not fluid. The statements of Scripture are absolute, and we are absolutely wrong to think that our personal or cultural experiences with God are our reference points for understanding his revelation.

10. Matthew 22:37, emphasis mine.

11. 1 Corinthians 2:4–5.

12. John 18:38.

13. The people groups least likely to believe in absolute moral truth are Baby Busters (those 36 and younger—only 13% embrace absolute truth), Catholics (16%), and adults who are not born-again Christians (15%). The groups most likely to endorse the existence of absolute moral truths include Baby Boomers (people 37 to 55 years of age—28% embrace absolute truth), adults who attend non-mainline Protestant churches (32%), and born-again individuals (32%) (*www.barna.org/FlexPage.aspx?Page=BarnaUpdate&BarnaUpdateID=102*).

14. *www.barna.org/FlexPage.aspx?Page=BarnaUpdate&BarnaUpdateID=162*.

15. Lamin O. Sanneh, *Whose Religion Is Christianity: The Gospel Beyond the West* (Grand Rapids: Eerdmans, 2003), 62.

16. Alan Wolfe, *Moral Freedom: The Search for Virtue in a World of Choice* (New York: W. W. Norton, 2001), 85ff.

17. Ibid., 220ff.

18. See William J. Bennett, *The Index of Leading Cultural Indicators: American Society at the End of the Twentieth Century* (New York: Broadway Books, 1999), and David Barton, *America: To Pray or Not to Pray* (Aledo, Tex.: WallBuilder Press, 1994).

19. Hosea 4:1–3.

20. Morpheus, in *The Matrix*.

21. Certainly, Jesus proclaimed the truth about God and life, but he refused to engage in technical discussions with religious leaders who wrangled over theological fine points: "'How terrible it will be for you teachers of religious law and you Pharisees. Hypocrites! For you are careful to tithe even the tiniest part of your income [in other words, "you write out your tithe checks to the penny"], but you ignore the important things of the law—justice, mercy, and faith. You should tithe, yes, but you should not leave undone the more important things. Blind guides! You strain your water so you won't accidentally swallow a gnat; then you swallow a camel'!" (Matthew 23:23–24 NLT).

22. See John 1:14, 17.

23. Pronounced ah-LAY-thay-ah, *alétheia* literally means "uncovered."

24. W. F. Arndt and F. W. Gingrich, *A Greek-English Lexicon of the New Testament* (Chicago: University of Chicago Press, 1957), 35–36, emphasis mine. The intended meaning of *alétheia* in the apostle John's gospel is undoubtedly shaped by the platonic view of the world as a mere shadow of reality.

25. John 1:9; 6:32; 15:1; 17:3. See C. H. Dodd, *The Interpretation of the Fourth Gospel* (Cambridge: Cambridge University Press, 1988), 139–40, 170.

26. John 4:23.
27. Dodd, 170.
28. All emphases mine.
29. John 17:17.
30. John 4:23–24.
31. John 8:32.
32. 1 John 1:6.
33. 1 John 1:8.
34. John 18:38.
35. John 14:6.
36. Regarding John 17:17, Dodd writes, "The *logos* [the Word, the divine truth] of Christ is the *logos* of God, and that is *alétheia, the ultimate reality revealed* (emphasis mine). . . . The divine *logos is alétheia.* That is to say, it is a rational content of thought corresponding to the ultimate reality of the universe" (267).
37. Hebrews 11:1 KJV.
38. 2 Corinthians 5:7.
39. *pisteuôn* followed by *eis* with the accusative case.
40. *pisteuôn* followed by *en* with the dative case.
41. See Dodd, 183.
42. See also 2:23 and 3:8.
43. Paraphrase of Numbers 14, 27.
44. Hebrews 3:19.
45. Genesis 22:6–8.
46. Then known as Mount Moriah.
47. See Exodus 3.
48. Emphasis mine.
49. See 1 Corinthians 7:29–31.
50. John 10:10 THE MESSAGE, emphasis mine.
51. See Joseph Ellis, *Founding Brothers: The Revolutionary Generation* (New York: Random House Vintage Books, 2000), 139.
52. Isaiah 33:6.
53. John 10:10 THE MESSAGE, emphasis mine.
54. Thomas à Kempis, *Following of Christ* (New York: Catholic Publications Press, 1925), 154.

CHAPTER THREE *The Cross 101*

1. For an online view, see *community.webshots.com/photo/52064757/52893397zajGGW.*
2. Thanks to Bill Hybels, who with his 2002 Easter message on bridges inspired me to preach on the same theme Easter 2003. My message became the basis for this chapter.
3. Psalm 19:1–2.

4. Psalm 19:3.
5. Genesis 11:4–5.
6. Romans 3:23, emphasis mine.
7. "The Great Divide," words and music by Grant Cunningham and Matt Huesmann, 1995.
8. A majority of Americans think that's in the Bible.
9. Romans 1:17, emphasis mine.
10. John 14:6.
11. Cunningham and Huesmann.
12. Horatio Spafford, "It Is Well With My Soul" (1873).
13. Roughly corresponding with *justification* and *sanctification,* respectively.
14. See Mark 8:34.
15. 1 Corinthians 1:18.
16. 1 Corinthians 2:2, emphasis mine.
17. 1 Corinthians 2:7–8.
18. Based on the Greek verb *agapaô;* the noun is *agapé.*
19. Matthew 10:39.
20. Matthew 5:5.
21. Galatians 5:24 NLT.

CHAPTER FOUR *The Passion Reloaded: More Blood Than a Mel Gibson Film*

1. John Stott, *The Cross of Christ* (Downers Grove, Ill.: InterVarsity, 1986), 43.
2. See *cross* in the *Dictionary of New Testament Theology,* Colin Brown, gen. ed. (Exeter, England: Paternoster, 1980).
3. "What is the largest religion in the world?" was a question on a 2002 *National Geographic* international geography survey of literacy. For more, visit *www.nationalgeographic.com.*
4. 1 Peter 1:1–2.
5. Luke 22:20 KJV, emphasis mine.
6. See Acts 20:13ff.
7. See John 1:29.
8. The sixth commandment—see Exodus 20:13.
9. Matthew 5:21–22.
10. Exodus 20:13.
11. Exodus 20:14.
12. Matthew 5:27–29.
13. 1 Corinthians 13:12 KJV.
14. Romans 3:23.
15. Greek *hémarton,* from *hamartánô.*
16. Micah 6:7.
17. Genesis 3:15.

18. Hebrews 10:1.
19. Greek *teleiôsai,* from *teleioô.*
20. Hebrews 10:5–6.
21. Hebrews 10:14.
22. Remember we're speaking of the word's general sense.
23. Arndt and Gingrich, 818.
24. John 19:30.
25. Hebrews 10:12, emphasis mine.
26. When used with "It is finished" and "made perfect."
27. The perfect tense signifies completed, past action with currently existing results.
28. Stott, 82.
29. Philippians 2:12–13.
30. I'm indebted for this statement to Dean Sherman, internationally known Youth With A Mission leader and teacher.
31. Jeremiah 31:33, "I will put my law in their minds and write it in their hearts."
32. Jeremiah 31:34, "I will remember their sins no more."
33. Hebrews 10:18, "No longer any sacrifice for sin."
34. John 6:54–55.
35. Luke 22:20.
36. Paraphrase of Exodus 12.

INTRODUCTION TO PART TWO
1. *http://kanaan.org/.*
2. See *www.cptryon.org/xpipassio/stations.*
3. John Piper, *The Passion of Jesus Christ* (Wheaton, Ill.: Crossway, 2004).
4. *www.dbu.edu/mitchell/crosswor.htm.*

CHAPTER FIVE *The Problem With Hell*
1. See Mark 9:43–48.
2. Romans 1:18; see also 2:5.
3. Genesis 2:17.
4. Romans 6:21–23, emphasis mine.
5. Matthew 27:46.
6. See 1 Peter 3:18–20.
7. John Calvin, as cited by Stott, 81.
8. 2 Corinthians 5:21.
9. Adapted from Peter Jensen, "The Good News of God's Wrath: At the Heart of the Universe, There Is a Just and Gracious God" in *Christianity Today,* March 2004, 46.
10. Meaning, guilt is *legal;* a guilty person doesn't have to feel guilty in order to be guilty.
11. Zechariah 3:4, emphasis mine.

12. Psalm 103:12.
13. John 1:29.
14. These are actual ancient uses of the Greek term *aphiémi,* most often translated "forgiveness." See also *aphesis.*
15. Zechariah 3:4.
16. See Matthew 25:41.
17. Judicial, forensic.
18. That is, being made right ("righteous," Greek *diakaiosuné*) with God.
19. Isaiah 53:4–6.
20. Matthew 1:20–21.
21. John 1:29.
22. Romans 3:23–25.
23. Matthew 27:46.
24. John 3:16.
25. Psalm 103:11–12.

CHAPTER SIX *Shame on You*

1. Romans 14:10.
2. John 16:8.
3. Genesis 2:25, emphasis mine.
4. You've probably noticed that it takes an absolute statement to deny all absolutes; this is an obvious problem for those who deny reality.
5. Genesis 3:7.
6. Psalm 38:4.
7. See Jeremiah 31:31.
8. Charles Moore, ed., *Provocations: Spiritual Writings of Kierkegaard* (Farmington, Pa.: The Plough Publishing House, 1999), 285.
9. Hebrews 10:18.
10. See also Galatians 2:21; 5:3–4.
11. Galatians 6:7–8.
12. See Psalm 103:12; Romans 8:38–39.
13. I "came down with a heart problem" as a result of an extraordinarily difficult year in the ministry, which I describe in more detail in my book coauthored with Alfred Ells, *Leaders That Last.* The only "cure" for cardiomyopathy is a heart transplant, but I'm pleased to say that, whatever was wrong with me at the time, I'm quite well today, some fifteen years later.
14. See 2 Corinthians 12:2ff.
15. Romans 11:22 KJV.
16. See John 14:16–17.
17. Arndt and Gingrich, 623.
18. Ephesians 4:15.
19. 2 Samuel 11:2–3, emphasis mine.

20. 2 Samuel 11:11, paraphrased.
21. 1 John 1:8–9.
22. See Leviticus 16.
23. Hebrews 10:19–20.
24. See Genesis 15.
25. *berit.*
26. Genesis 15:17–18.
27. Luke 22:19.
28. The Hebrew word for *covenant* (*berit*) and the Greek equivalent (*diatheke*) "rarely denote a two-sided, contractual agreement between partners of equal standing. *Berit* is used almost without exception for a one-sided obligation, albeit one that has a pledge attached. Accordingly it is often connected with the taking of an oath or blood rite conditioned by a curse on one's self. . . . The *berit* theology of the Old Testament is based upon the idea of royal sovereignty. The king's own obligation to bestow on his servants kindness, faithfulness, protection, and care precede the covenant obligation of his subjects. . . . In all instances [where the *berit* concept appears in the Old Testament] the emphasis lies on irrevocable commitment" (*Exegetical Dictionary of the New Testament,* Vol. I [Grand Rapids: Eerdmans, 1978–1980], 299).
29. Some Christians participate in the Seder meal also; the Jewish ceremony is filled with spiritually meaningful symbols for the Christian.
30. Hebrews 10:23.
31. Hebrews 10:24.
32. See Philippians 2:12–13; the literal translation of "you have been saved" in Ephesians 2:8 is "you are *having been* saved" (Greek *este sesôsmenoi,* perfect passive participle).
33. Ephesians 2:10.
34. Hebrews 10:25.
35. *The Barna Report,* November/December 1997.
36. There are, of course, believers who are phenomenally different, who've been radically changed and have grown in faith, who are passionately committed and set apart, but our cultural matrix has many Christ-followers in its grip, and it keeps trying to seduce all of us.
37. Hebrews 10:19–22.
38. Psalm 32:5.
39. Hebrews 9:9, 14.
40. Ephesians 1:7–8.
41. Luke 23:34.
42. Colossians 1:22.
43. Romans 8:1.

CHAPTER SEVEN *Slaves*

1. F. F. Bruce, *Paul: Apostle of the Heart Set Free* (Grand Rapids: Eerdmans, 1977).
2. Also known as "The War of the Rebellion" and "The War Between the States."
3. "Battle Hymn of the Republic," words by Julia Ward Howe, emphasis mine.
4. See Numbers 11:5.
5. Romans 6:11.
6. Ephesians 4:26.
7. 2 Corinthians 12:10.
8. See Romans 6:1–2.
9. 1 John 1:8.
10. There is no exact English equivalent.
11. Romans 6:12–14 THE MESSAGE.
12. 1 John 1:9, emphasis mine.
13. See Galatians 2:20.
14. See Lamentations 3:22–23.
15. M. Scott Peck, *People of the Lie* (New York: Simon and Schuster, 1983).
16. The sacrament of confession is commonly known as penance.
17. James 5:16.
18. Gary Kinnaman and Alfred Ells, *Leaders That Last* (Grand Rapids: Baker, 2003).
19. See Genesis 2:18.
20. Matthew 18:20, emphasis mine.
21. Galatians 1:3–4.
22. Romans 8:2–4.
23. Romans 8:8–10.
24. Romans 6:6–11.
25. John 19:28.
26. Romans 6:12–14.
27. Romans 6:16–17.

CHAPTER EIGHT *Yes, Virginia, There Is a Devil*

1. Gary D. Kinnaman, *Winning Your Spiritual Battles: How to Use the Full Armor of God* (Ann Arbor: Servant/Vine, 2003).
2. To use a biblical term; see 2 Corinthians 10:4.
3. Neil T. Anderson, *Victory Over the Darkness* (Ventura, Calif.: Regal, 2000); Neil T. Anderson, *The Bondage Breaker* (Eugene, Ore.: Harvest House, 2000); Neil T. Anderson, with Timothy M. Warner, *Beginner's Guide to Spiritual Warfare* (Ann Arbor: Servant/Vine, 2000). Also, M. Scott Peck's *People of the Lie: The Hope for Healing Human Evil* (New York: Simon and Schuster, 1983), in which he makes a case for demon

possession and deliverance (remarkably rare in his profession [psychiatry]). Finally, C. Fred Dickason, *Demon Possession and the Christian* (Chicago: Moody, 1987).

4. Ephesians 4:26–27, emphasis mine.
5. See Phillip Jenkins, *The Next Christendom: The Coming of Global Christianity* (New York: Oxford University Press, 2003).
6. Harvey Cox, *Fire From Heaven: The Rise of Pentecostal Spirituality and the Reshaping of Religion in the 21st Century* (New York: Addison-Wesley, 1995).
7. 1 John 3:8.
8. 1 Peter 5:8–9, emphasis mine.
9. See Colossians 2:14–15.
10. See Romans 13:1–7.
11. See Psalm 122:6.
12. Revelation 13:3–4, 6–7, emphasis mine; you may wish to read all of Revelation 13 for context.
13. Mount Doom is a seat of evil in *Lord of the Rings*. Also, read Revelation 17.
14. Luke 16:13.
15. See Hebrews 13:5; in light of this, read Revelation 18.
16. Psalm 2:1–4; also read Revelation 19.
17. Proverbs 1:7; 3:6.
18. Isaiah 9:6–7, emphasis mine; see also Psalm 2:9.
19. See 2 Corinthians 10:4–5.
20. Colossians 1:13–14.
21. Colossians 2:14–15.
22. 1 John 3:8.
23. Acts 26:17–18.
24. Luke 23:46.
25. 2 Corinthians 4:3–4.
26. Acts 10:38.

CHAPTER NINE *Going Nowhere Fast*

1. Howard Bingham (interviewer and author of *Muhammad Ali: A Thirty-Year Journey*), "Ali," *Reader's Digest* (Dec. 2001), 93.
2. James 2:10.
3. See Matthew 5:21–22.
4. See Matthew 5:27–30.
5. Matthew 5:20.
6. See John 3:1–5.
7. John 3:16.
8. Isaiah 64:6, emphasis added.
9. Luke 7:47.

10. Galatians 5:4.
11. Galatians 5:4 TLB.
12. Galatians 5:4 THE MESSAGE.
13. Romans 8:1–4.
14. Romans 10:3–5; cf. Leviticus 18:5.
15. Romans 13:8–10.
16. 1 Corinthians 15:56–57.
17. See John 19:25–27.
18. Galatians 3:10–14.
19. Galatians 2:16.
20. Galatians 2:19–21.

CHAPTER TEN Extreme Life

1. John 10:10 KJV, emphasis mine.
2. Arndt and Gingrich, 657.
3. 1 Timothy 6:19.
4. Arndt and Gingrich, 340–41.
5. Colossians 1:27.
6. See Genesis 11:1–9.
7. 1 Peter 2:9.
8. Ephesians 2:14.
9. Karen Patterson, "Why Is Everyone So Short-Tempered?" *USA Today,* July 18, 2000.
10. Scott Russell Sanders, *Writing From the Center* (Bloomington, Ind.: Indiana University Press, 1995), 72–73.
11. Robert D. Putnam, *Bowling Alone: The Collapse and Revival of American Community* (New York: Simon and Schuster, 2000), 253.
12. Putnam, 204.
13. Acts 17:26, emphasis mine.
14. I highly recommend Scott Russell Sanders' book *Staying Put,* which I referenced earlier. (*Staying Put: Making a Home in a Restless World* [Boston: Beacon, 1993].)
15. Putnam, 232–41.
16. Cox, *Fire From Heaven.*
17. See 1 Corinthians 1:18.
18. I don't know the precise ratio, but our intake of these medications is vastly disproportionate to the rest of the world.
19. As he was reviewing my manuscript, my most excellent editor, Christopher Soderstrom, let me know in no uncertain terms that he is a "monstrous Vikings fan" and that he "can't remember the last time we surrendered 50." [Ed's note: 1984.] Okay, then, maybe I'm exaggerating, but I remember it was a shameful loss.
20. Proverbs 9:10; cf. Psalm 111:10.

21. Luke 14:27.

22. Doug Pagitt, interview in LEADERSHIP (Fall 2002), 33.

23. Randy Alcorn, *Money, Possessions, and Eternity* (Wheaton, Ill.: Tyndale, 1993, rev. ed. 2003), 413–14.

24. "No man can serve two masters: for either he will hate the one, and love the other; or else he will hold to the one, and despise the other. Ye cannot serve God and mammon" (Matthew 6:24 KJV).

25. Gerhard Kittel, *Theological Dictionary of the New Testament*, Vol. IV, trans. Geoffrey Bromiley (Grand Rapids: Eerdmans, 1967), 389.

26. Alcorn, 414.

27. Galatians 3:14.

28. Romans 6:6–8.

29. Isaiah 53:4–5.

30. 1 Peter 2:24–25.

31. Luke 23:40–43, emphasis mine.

32. Matthew 8:16–17.

33. John 11:25–26.

CHAPTER ELEVEN *Beyond Extreme Life*

1. *www.barna.org/FlexPage.aspx?Page=BarnaUpdate&BarnaUpdateID=150.*

2. *www.drudgereport.com.*

3. M. Scott Peck, *Further Along the Road Less Traveled* (New York: Simon and Schuster, 1993), 51.

4. Hans Küng, *Eternal Life?*, trans. Edward Quin (New York: Crossroad: 1991), 162.

5. Ernest Becker, *The Denial of Death* (New York: The Free Press, 1973), 13ff.

6. Jonathan Edwards, from *The Great Christian Doctrine of Original Sin.*

7. Robert Morey, *Death and the Afterlife* (Minneapolis: Bethany House, 1984), 40, emphasis mine.

8. 1 Corinthians 15:20.

9. 1 Corinthians 15:58.

10. Peck, *Further Along the Road Less Traveled*, 47.

11. 1 Thessalonians 4:16–18, emphasis mine.

12. Adapted from Morey, 40.

13. Ecclesiastes 3:1ff.

14. Romans 6:8–10.

15. 1 Corinthians 15:21–23.

16. 1 Corinthians 15:24–26.

17. 2 Timothy 1:8–10.

18. John 19:30, emphasis mine.

19. 1 Corinthians 3:21–23.

20. 1 Corinthians 15:54–58.

CHAPTER TWELVE *Scandalous Freedom*
1. Arndt and Gingrich, 760.
2. Luke 6:28.
3. Greek *agapé;* see 1 Corinthians 13.
4. Paraphrased; see 1 Corinthians 1:10–13; 2:2; 3:1–3.
5. 1 Corinthians 1:18–25.
6. Philippians 2:3.
7. Philippians 2:5–7.
8. Philippians 2:4.
9. Al Ells, a dear friend, is coauthor with me of *Leaders That Last* (Grand Rapids: Baker, 2003).
10. Matthew 21:5 KJV.
11. 1 Peter 3:7.
12. Ephesians 5:24.
13. See Ephesians 6:1–3.
14. Ephesians 6:4.
15. Colossians 4:1.
16. Colossians 3:22–24.
17. James 4:10.
18. Matthew 5:44, 46–47; Luke 6:35, 37.
19. Luke 6:35–38.
20. See Matthew 5:25.
21. Hebrews 13:4.
22. See 1 Timothy 6:10 and Hebrews 13:5.
23. Luke 16:13–14.
24. Luke 6:29–30
25. Cf. Isaiah 53:3.
26. *www.oxymoronica.com.*
27. Alan E. Nelson, *Broken in the Right Place* (Nashville: Thomas Nelson, 1994).
28. Matthew 21:44.
29. John 12:24.
30. *home.arcor.de/goodreligion/good/lyrics/brokenness.*
31. Richard J. Foster, *Prayer: Finding the Heart's True Home* (HarperSanFrancisco, 1992), 62–63.

CHAPTER THIRTEEN *The Scandal of Forgiveness*
1. Technically, Birkenau, a vast secondary camp constructed to accommodate the original, smaller barracks at Auschwitz.
2. Arguably the most powerful and renowned passage in holocaust literature, Wiesel's first book, *Night,* records the inclusive experience of the Jews from which this text was taken, and he has since dedicated his life to ensuring that none of us forget what happened to the Jews. Wiesel

survived Auschwitz, Buna, Buchenwald, and Gleiwitz. After the liberation of the camps in April 1945, he spent a few years in a French orphanage, began to study in Paris at the Sorbonne, and became involved in journalistic work with the French newspaper *L'arche*. Nobel laureate François Mauriac eventually influenced Wiesel to break his vowed silence and write of his experience in the concentration camps, thus beginning a lifetime of service. Wiesel has since published over thirty books, earned the Nobel Peace Prize, been appointed to chair the President's Commission on the Holocaust, awarded the Congressional Gold Medal of Achievement, and more.

3. Dennis Prager, "The Sin of Forgiveness," *The Wall Street Journal* (Dec. 15, 1997).

4. Jeffrie G. Murphy, *Getting Even: Forgiveness and Its Limits* (New York: Oxford University Press, 2003), dust jacket.

5. James 5:16.

6. Ephesians 4:26.

7. Hebrews 12:15.

8. *www.forgivenessinstitute.org*.

9. See Genesis 37.

10. See 1 Corinthians 5:1–7.

11. See 2 Corinthians 12:7–10.

12. 1 Peter 2:23.

13. Scott Heller, *The Chronicle of Higher Education* (July 1998), 18–19.

14. Ibid. p. 19.

15. From an extraordinary article on the emerging secular research on the benefits of forgiveness by David Van Biema and Wendy Cole, "Should All Be Forgiven?" *Time* (April 5, 1999).

16. Lewis B. Smedes, *Forgive and Forget: Healing the Hurts We Don't Deserve* (San Francisco: Harper and Row, 1984), 29.

17. Matthew 6:12.

18. Luke 23:42–43.

19. Luke 23:34.

20. Matthew 6:12, paraphrased.

21. Luke 22:44.

22. Matthew 26:42.

23. From Philip Yancey, "The Unnatural Act," *Christianity Today* (April 8, 1991).

24. Hebrews 11:1 KJV.

25. Luke 17:3–4.

26. David Augsburger, *The "F" Word: Forgiveness and Its Imitations,* an interview in *Steps* (Fall 1997), 6.

27. See Matthew 18:21–22.

28. Luke 17:5.

29. Luke 6:28.

30. David Manuel, *Bosnia: Hope in the Ashes* (Brewster, Mass.: Paraclete Press, 1996), 89–91.

31. Derived from a National Public Radio audio recording of a discussion on the dynamics of forgiveness, with host Ray Suarez on "Talk of the Nation" (April 20, 1999), with guests Frederic Luskin, Director of the Forgiveness Project at Stanford University; Fr. Drew Christiansen, senior fellow at the Woodstock Theological Center at Georgetown University and co-editor of *Peacemaking: Moral and Policy Challenges for a New World;* and John Borneman, author of *Settling Accounts: Violence, Justice, and Accountability in Postsocialist Europe.*

32. See Matthew 18:21–35.

33. See Ephesians 6:10ff.

34. Ephesians 6:12 THE MESSAGE.

35. Lewis B. Smedes, *The Art of Forgiving: When You Need to Forgive and Don't Know How* (Nashville: Moorings, 1996).

36. Everett L. Worthington, *Forgiving and Reconciling: Bridges to Wholeness and Hope* (Downers Grove, Ill.: InterVarsity, 2003).

37. Lewis B. Smedes, *Forgive and Forget.*